The Return of Heaven on Earth

Messages to Awaken Peace, Hope, and Joy in the Midst of Monumental Change

Channeled Messages & Personal Reflection Journal

Karen J. Vivenzio

Copyright © 2023 by Karen J. Vivenzio

All rights reserved. No part of this book may be used or reproduced by any means, graphic, electronic, or mechanical, including photocopying, recording, taping or by any information storage retrieval system without the written permission of the author except in the case of brief quotations embodied in critical articles or reviews.

The author of this book does not dispense medical advice or prescribe the use of any technique as a form of treatment for physical, emotional, or medical problems without the advice of a physician, either directly or indirectly. The intent of the author is only to offer information of a general nature to help you in your quest for quest for emotional and spiritual well-being. In the event you use any of the information in this book for yourself, which is your constitutional right, the author and the publisher assume no responsibility for your actions.

e-Book ISBN: 978-1-960815-10-1

Paperback ISBN: 978-1-960815-11-8

Hardcover ISBN: 978-1-960815-12-5

Published by: Book Writer Corner 2023

Dedicated to:

A Global Intervention for the Spiritual Ascension of Humankind.

Healing the World One Soul at a Time.

CONTENTS

Acknowledgment i
Introduction 1
About the Messengers 6
Messages and Reflection Journal 10
You are the Stars that Shine in Your Own Hearts and Minds 11
Change is Upon You 17
You are the Harbingers of Times to Come 21
Time to Carry the Highest Vibe 24
Embracing a Higher Way of Life 30
Recovery Set In Motion 35
You are the Most Powerful Transformative Force in the Universe 38
Step into a Brand New Way of Life 42
Shedding the Cloak of Fear 46
Time for Forgiveness 50
The Forces of Love will Rise 55
You are a Beacon, So Shine Your Light 59
Emerging from Fear and Disharmony 63
Stopping the Program of Fear 66
Connect to the God Self Within Thee 70
The Great Shift is Taking Place 76

Preparing You to Take Flight 82

Blessings Flowing on the Incoming Tide 85

Welcoming the Blessing Times 91

Tune In 95

A Journey of Rebirth 102

Rebirth of Heaven on Earth 107

Breathe in the Essence of What is Next 111

Allow Your Hearts to Open Up 118

All is Being Brought to Light 122

The Heart of Creation Calling You Forth 129

Release Yourselves from the Shackles of Doom 135

Change will Come in Whispers and Everlasting Grace 140

Hold onto Your Light 145

You are the Beacon; You are the Light 150

Life is an Inside Game 154

Allow Infinite Changes to Take Place 160

Time for Letting Go 164

Witnessing the End of the Play 169

Merge into a New Understanding of Holiness 175

Finding the Oneness in You 180

Listen to the Holy Spark Deep Inside You 186

You Have Always Been Whole and Complete 190

The Gap is Closing Between Heaven and Earth 194

Change is in the Air 200

Streamers of Love from Our Hearts to Yours 207

Reach Forward, Rise Above 214

Time to Resurrect the Dreams You Left Behind 219

You are the Light of a Thousand Suns 224

The Veil has been Pierced and the Convergence Begun 229

The Universe is an Infinite Canvas on which to Create 234

You are Leaps and Bounds from Where You Started Out 239

We are Holding You 244

Waiting for Your Hearts to Re-Align 248

The Creation Spins Again and Again 253

Grand New Opening 256

The Time has Come to Unveil the Secret Ones 259

Heaven is Waiting for You with Open Arms 263

The Light is Working Overtime Right Now 268

Timelines Converging 275

Entering the Center of Universal Rebirth 281

The End of One Age and the Entering of the Next 287

The Heavens have Opened a Spirit of Grace 292

Breath in the Newness, Set Your Intention 299

Keep the Lamp of Faith Well Lit 305

Hold the Light of Unconditional Love 310

The New Dimension is Now in Sight 314

Allow Your Soul to Blossom, Bloom, and Grow 319

Uncover the Magic that is about to Unfold 323

Honor the Cycle of Clearing and Healing 329

The Clouds have Disappeared 336

Emerging from the Cocoon 343

Living in a Virtual Reality 348

Breathe Healing into the World 353

On the Precipice of the Great Return 358

Speak Your Truth and Rejoice 364

Infinite Possibilities Surround You Now 370

The Sacred Script of Your Brand New Life 375

Life is Not a War to be Fought 379

The Curve has been Turned 390

The Slate is Wiped Clean 397

Hope is on the Horizon 401

You are the Beacons of Hope 407

Clearing of the Debris 414

Savor the Newness that Surrounds You 418

Clearing of the Shadows 425

Hold the Light 432

Holy Dispensation to Lighten the Road Ahead 436

Welcome To the Glorious, Gracious, Loving Light 439

Season of Blessings Moving Within You 444

United in Peace and Grace 449

Acknowledgment

I am so grateful to my angels and spiritual guides along with Mother Divine and the Legions of Light for their heartfelt messages full of love and blessings which they desire to communicate to all of humanity. This book would not have been possible without the help of many helpers and friends on Earth and in Heaven. May the gift of these words spread much peace, love, and understanding to all people everywhere.

Introduction

By all accounts, the past few years have been challenging ones, with the worldwide pandemic, turmoil in the financial markets, and the continual threat of war, this has arguably been one of the most difficult times in recent history for many people. And yet, in the preceding century, we made it through two world wars and many other periods of famine and disease, and, despite it all, humanity is still standing. Yet we need some hope and inspiration to fill our hearts with love and joy and to rebuild relationships with ourselves and others after going through what many have called a great hibernation period.

Many of us are wondering where God is during this time of change; many of us are feeling empty, lost and do not know which way to turn. As I was thinking about this today, an insight came to me that I wanted to share with you as I think it is most important to be able to look at this time not as a time of despair and loss but as an opportunity for amazing positive change.

Right now, what we are experiencing is void. It is a time when everything around us has stopped, and most of us are being challenged in many ways – emotionally, physically, and spiritually. Our ties to the communities around us are being challenged. Many of us are on the front lines of this virus and witnessing the ravages on the human bodies, patients in isolation without family or friends allowed to visit. Others of us are in isolation of our own making, in our houses, and alone with our thoughts. The world as we know it has stopped for a time, allowing us the opportunity to pause and assess and rebuild. This is a reboot of sorts for each and every one of us. It is a time of gathering new ideas, sifting through them to see which makes the most sense, learning and leaning on one another, even if over the phone or the zoom call on the computer, gathering our energies and our senses before we once again begin to create.

THE REBIRTH OF HEAVEN ON EARTH

This is the empty space where God begins to fill you up, with new ideas, with love and hope and peace and grace. This is Angel's space within every one of us, a sacred space that has opened and needs to be filled with harmony and a new, more positive vision for our world. This is the space the Holy Spirit is waiting for, within each of us, for our higher purpose to be fulfilled, and She whispers: "LOVE each other - that is all that counts, being in a state of LOVE - nothing else."

God has not disappeared. This is the time that God is washing us clean of all that no longer serves us, wiping off the tarnish and filling us with sparkle, glitter that shines for our new priorities in this game called life. Though it looks like something else, this is the time of God, the time of goodness, of healing from where we have been, getting us ready for the new - getting us ready to step into a new world; the peace and blessings of heaven on earth.

THE REBIRTH OF HEAVEN ON EARTH

So take time in silence each day and call in a blessing, call in prayer to God, the Holy Spirit, Mother Divine, the Angels, and the Legions of Light. These beings are not relegated to any one religion, belief system, or tribe. They act in service to humanity as a whole to lift us up from where we have been and to help us begin again. Everyone is worthy of their guidance and support. So ask them to fill you up; to fill that space deep within with the blessings of love, the blessings of hope and peace and joy – and know that your prayers have been heard, that the Angels of Heaven are welcoming you into their realm – the brand new realm of heaven on earth and that nothing like these prayers have ever before been heard – the prayer of angels on earth welcoming in the blessings of goodness and grace and the smiles that light up on every human being's face. It is a time of welcoming in respect for all who seek the pleasures and blessings bestowed upon the meek.

THE REBIRTH OF HEAVEN ON EARTH

It is from a deep space of healing and going within to reflect on God, the Holy Spirit, and all that is good in this world that I have decided to share these amazing words of wisdom I have received in prayer over the last 4 years. These are direct messages from Mother Divine, the Angels, and the Legions of Light brought forth with love, light, and blessings from my heart to yours.

Each day allow yourself to select a message that is relevant to you and read, reflect, and journal about what it means for you. May you receive much hope and inspiration from reflecting on these divine messages, and may the blessings contained within allow your hearts and souls to breathe in new life, creating a miracle of sunshine in your everyday lives. Together we will welcome the rebirth of heaven on earth.

Peace and Bright Blessings - Karen

About the Messengers

Many messengers from heaven have stepped forward to assist humanity during this time of tremendous change. Some of them you may know and some you may discover through the blessed messages included here.

The Legions of Light are the benevolent angels, archangels, spiritual masters and guides who have been known in the many religious and spiritual belief systems throughout the world. Jesus, Buddha, amd Archangel Michael are examples of the magnificent beings of light that belong to this team in spriit. They, along with Mother Divine, have come forward to assist humanity to find their way back to love during this time of significant transition.

Mother Divine is called by many names. Her presence is found in traditional religions and many varied belief systems across the globe. To the Jewish people, she is Shekinah—the presence of God that lives within. To the

Christians, she is the Holy Ghost, the Holy Spirit, Divine Mother, or Mother God. The Hindus call her Shakti. The Native Americans and other aboriginal people refer to her as Great Mother, Mother Earth, Mother Nature, or Mother Moon, depending on the tribe. In more recent spiritual or esoteric belief systems, she is simply known as the Divine Feminine or the higher, most nurturing aspects of ourselves.

Though the names vary by culture, her role appears the same. In all of these belief systems, she represents the mother or female aspect of God. While the male God many of us have been trained to know represents the external, outer qualities of strength, power, and control of the Father; the female divine represents the introspective, quiet aspects of creativity, personal connection, and unconditional love of the Mother. God, in my view, is both feminine and masculine, a perfect balance of inner and outer strength. The Mother (divine feminine) and Father (divine masculine) are each just one aspect of the entire whole.

The messages that have been sent from their hearts to mine are filled with love and joy, a comforting sense of parental guidance, and higher insight that, at times, leaves me amazed and breathless with the beauty and grace of the words as they flow onto the page.

There is always a higher order, a transcendent way to view who we are and our place in this ever-challenging world. Mother Divine's messages, along with those from the angelic realm, and the benevolent legions of light, are for everyone regardless of their own personal religious or spiritual beliefs.

As you reflect on these words, take the time to let them seep in – soak in them, breathe them in, read the messages again and again, and you will find you find new meaning each time you do. These words are a gift from God. They do not need to be read in any specific order. There is not just one truth and each message may mean something different to each person that reads it. Take what you like and what makes sense to you. May you find in these healing messages much peace and hope.

Messages

and

Reflection Journal

You are the Stars that Shine in Your Own Hearts and Minds

Child of light, your children are safe with us tonight. We surround and protect all whom you ask, for we are the guardians of the light waiting for change to come to pass so that all will know within their souls that the light shines bright and their destiny is to SHINE their light.

For you are a beacon of which you know not the power that you hold. You are on the verge of becoming ever more bold. We cannot wait to see the light that you now begin to shine as you are on the verge of breaking through the membrane covering you in lies (shroud covered in lies) - removal of the veil that separates the two worlds, imminent change and embracing you all. For you are our family, we are one with you in the name of love, the vibration of love that shines between all souls - all humanity and across the globe. Shine bright your light, and know this, dear child, we are one with you and have been all the while you thought you were alone; we were standing there before you holding you close.

Wrapped in bright wings of sparkling light, embracing you, dear child, throughout the darkest of nights, rejoicing with you in the springtime rain and sending you solace and sights of dismay.

For you are the light that shines in the rain, and we are the way showers leading the path home. For in reality, your home is the universe itself, the blanket of light that connects us all, leading you home, leading you home. Global family ready for quite a show, opening occurring, lifting you up into the universal consciousness of love, love, love. Stars are shining brightly within your very own souls, reaching the outer limits of the membrane now, expanding beyond the confines you have never known, expanding and reaching for the stars, for soon you will realize they are not very far, for they are reflections of your own true hearts. In fact, all of us, that is what we really are, reflections in the midst of the perceptive shift, sparkling light, sparkling bright.

Revealing to you now, the message is this, learn to live in the midst of your own sweet bliss - for you are the creators of the world to come, reflect and resolve all that is left undone, for completion is imminent as the new world creation has already begun.

Leave behind all that no longer serves and step into the opportunities of a brand new world.

For what surrounds you now will not be for long, you are walking into a brand new world of opportunities, and it has already begun. New life, new soul, a new place to call home, the Earth is shining brighter than ever before. Never before, never before, have the options looked so bright, shining like the stars that appear in your hearts and minds, for you have the power to turn on the lights and make it all right. Turning the tides of life in despair into one of grace and power, for you are a reflection of the Creator, my dear, one and the same. The Creator and you, the reflection of the light of the universe, are already in you.

Access it now, turn on the flames, light shining through the darkest of days, fueling you forward in the name of the light; the love you have blessed to others now becomes your birthright. To have and to hold the dreams that you cherish, manifesting the blessings now through all who seek a brighter world and a better life for Thee.

For you are the beacon of love creating through Me, the divine light of love, that is what to see reflected in the creations that abound in the name of sweet Victory. For I

AM the one for which you seek the higher frequency of light bounding through infinity.

In love and grace and blessings bestowed, I AM the Victory within your bright soul. For I AM one with the light, and I AM Your Sweet Mother Divine.

What does this message mean to you?

What action or feelings does this inspire in you?

How can you bring the wisdom of this message into your daily life?

Change is Upon You

Dearest child, change is upon you; change is coming through you, in you, and all around you. The limitations that you have set for yourselves are being dissolved, drawing away the darkness of unknowing and bringing forth the light of wisdom to keep you company for a while.

Dearest of hearts, yours is so bright; we wish you could see the light from which you shine.

For you have made an impact on many a life, so silent and humble is your name, but we know it well, for the heart speaks more than words could ever say. Our heart and your heart are one and the same, for we are not all different but simply different aspects of one and the same. Great fortunes have been stored up in your great name, and soon you will see the pouring forth of a new destiny.

For you have all graduated and are moving in a great new direction. There are millions upon millions of stars showering you with blessings. We are the lights that shine upon darkness itself, the ones you have been talking about. We are the galactic beings of light, the angels, the masters, and the spiritual guides. The collective of wisdom where wisdom resides, deep in the heart of your own dear minds.

The vibration of light sings a sweet song. Hold onto the moment, remember these times of struggle and wonder and watch as they give way to a big clap of thunder – applause from above and below, the beings unseen, and the end of quite a magical show, for you have done it dearest children of mine, you have done the deeds we cannot deny – to wake up in the morning full of new light, seeing the world itself in a brand new light.

THE REBIRTH OF HEAVEN ON EARTH

For we have hemmed and hawed and pushed you forth, and you have responded in kindness and mercy, moving forward, moving forward. I wish to tell you now, dearest children of mine, that you are the vibration creating new light. You are the generators, the weight bearers of the tribe, the angelic human-divine creating more light.

Like flames on the beaches or shells blazing bright, the sun shines its brilliance on the tribe of light, creating new life, creating new life.

Your Father, Your Mother, Mary, and Me
(Archangel Michael)

What does this message mean to you?

What action or feelings does this inspire in you?

How can you bring the wisdom of this message into your daily life?

THE REBIRTH OF HEAVEN ON EARTH

You are the Harbingers of Times to Come

You are each and every soul reading this message, the harbingers of times to come. Change is coming fast across your lands, and the Earth is singing praises for She has been waiting for so many, many years to make the leap across the stage that is, in fact, the final end of this sad play.

No more songs to be sung about war and war-torn lands to be reclaimed for the highest good. For we say to you now, dear sweet children of light, you are the members of the human, angelic tribe.

Many have come before you, but never have so many shined so bright, reaching out into the hearts of the infinite universal mind. Hearts are shining bright as the stars that shine, now is your time.

THE REBIRTH OF HEAVEN ON EARTH

It is time to stand up and be counted, letting all you think you know to be pushed aside and become the vehicles to carry only the highest of vibes. For so many of you are ready to stand in the light, yet knowing not what you might find come daylight.

For in darkness so long, you long to belong, but my darlings, you were born to sing your own song. Your vibration is so high, standing unwavering in the bright sun.

Let us fill you with our love, angel wings wrapped around you so tight, filling you full with the brightest of life. Breathing new life into the war-weary souls. Blessing the entire world.

The Angel Collective singing to you today

What does this message mean to you?

What action or feelings does this inspire in you?

How can you bring the wisdom of this message into your daily life?

Time to Carry the Highest Vibe

Dearest children of light and all those who desire a better life, it is now time to carry the highest of vibes, to walk humanity over the threshold of a new life.

For a new play awaits. The stage is now set to carry you through the waves of fear into the blessings of love flowing in from above.

For we are beaming great light into your hearts and minds.

Nothing you find will ever be the same as the war-torn weary world you see before you now. The illusion has been broken; the spell no longer holds you, for you have learned to see a higher level of truth. And now we ask you to rise above, never mind, the games being played in the political realm; it is up to you to create a higher wave, transcending the frequency of drama and shame into the octave of dreams to reclaim.

For the wisdom of the elders is shining so bright, so many are holding for you the vibration of light. It is time for you to delve deep inside, into the heart of the infinite mind. All that you need is inside you, my dears.

All that you need to keep you away from fear.

For fear is the poison that lies between the lines. It is fear that keeps you from embracing your own sweet light. Open your heart and your mind, and resolve to find common ground to unite the remnants of illusion still flowing through you.

Invoke the violet flame of dear St. Germain to burn away the dross and the worldly concerns, for even now, we see you caught up in the dramas before you. You must let all the drama go. You must refuse to let even one remnant of darkness remain in your world.

You are the ones you have been waiting for. We have been holding the space for you, but now you know what you must do. In peace and light, in the stillness of the night, release the remaining vestiges of the play and walk onto the brand-new stage.

New lights have been set; a new script is in hand. Dare to take the highest road to the destiny you seek.

For you were born to make a difference. You were born to share your light. It matters not the names that you seek or the glory to be reaped. What matters is the vibe and frequency you use to create the notions of love and to transform all the hate.

THE REBIRTH OF HEAVEN ON EARTH

For no one can move forward without the shore to stand them tall, and no one can embrace the love of the mountain without having to climb it at all.

To embrace and be loved is the essence of life, so fill yourself full of blessings this time.

For you will not fail, you have come so far; the moment is near when all will be shown, the curtains reveal the illusion, and then, seeds will be planted to begin once again. Full of new promise, new hope to behold, a barren land filled with the wildflowers of your souls. The wonders you seek are set to be yours. Sharing and blessing each other with love, compassion, and the promise of the abundance of love.

We are the way showers, the warriors of peace, and we come to you now in infinite need. To grace the world with our presence and shower the Divine with the love of the great changing of tides.

We are Archangel Michael, and the Legions of Light come to you now in the darkest of times to let you know of the changing tides and the blessings becoming from the Infinite Light.

What does this message mean to you?

What action or feelings does this inspire in you?

How can you bring the wisdom of this message into your daily life?

Embracing a Higher Way of Life

Dearest hearts, we wish to speak to you tonight about the impending changes taking flight.

For you have waited so long in such an infinite fight for the wrongs to become now right. So many of you have shifted the vibe, and it is time to welcome you back into the light. That does not mean you have to leave your earthly vessels; on the contrary, you are welcoming your higher selves into the earthly plane to help you learn to love again.

It is from this higher perspective that you will see the old truths no longer hold true.

For this is a new day, a new dawn has come, stepping into oneness and love. There is no greater mission, no greater feat, than transcending the world of poverty and lack and finding your way back to the light of abundance and grace and sweet love. These are the gifts to be restored to your dear ones.

For so many have waited with great faith in their Lords, never knowing the tools were inside you all along. By turning your focus inward, you will become the Infinite Ones. So full of light and love and hope that no one can ever doubt the existence of what they have not been able to see until now.

For you are the ones to start the new show. New script in hand, let go of all you currently know. New truths to come out quite swiftly, it's clear, to show the masses a triumphant and luminous pathway from fear to redemption, from our hearts to yours, a unification of all that has come before.

The dimensions are closing in on themselves, uniting the energies – weaving a new tapestry for this game you call life.

For in the higher realms, we watch, and we think, how do they take themselves so seriously?

For what you see before you is only one aspect of you.

For you are so much more than this one life, you are one of many 'yous' in many dimensions of time. You can never know the glory you have brought to this life.

For you cannot see your infinite light. You do not yet know the full wisdom inside. But now we will show you the higher vibrations of light to move into the dimensions that house the reflections of the highest of mind.

THE REBIRTH OF HEAVEN ON EARTH

Shine bright, shine bright, children divine, for we are your brothers and sisters in the infinite light, and we are here to show you what it means to recover your life/light.

Blessings Divine, We are the Legions of Light, and I AM Archangel Michael at one with the light

What does this message mean to you?

What action or feelings does this inspire in you?

How can you bring the wisdom of this message into your daily life?

Recovery Set In Motion

Dearest children, walk not in anger or fright but in the joyful knowing that change is coming just down the pike. Soon you will realize all of your needs are always met. There is no illusion that can keep you from us tonight, only the fearful vibe that not all is right.

All is well.

Destiny comes in many ways, shapes, and forms, dear one. We hope you know that all will be fulfilled as has been planned since the beginning. It was always meant that heaven would remain on earth for all eternity - the recovery has been set in motion, and nothing will stop what the hearts and minds of so many have put forth in intention and grace - there will be smiles on sweet angels' faces - just a few more miles to go, through the fog of darkness before the tunnel gives way to sweet surprises.

Much is in store which you have not yet learned. It will be up to you to control the pace at which the new flows forth. By way of your intention and setting your beliefs aside, for what you have been taught is not at all how the world thrives. Keep in mind all that has come through the power of your own heart to transmute and transform the energy of light, and know now, this dearest child of mine; you are more than what you see. In fact, you are the bridge to infinity – infinite light playing a multitude of games, en-joy and en-lighten the stage today.

With peace, love, and laughter, we stand by your side, for I AM Your Mother Divine, and you are ALL my Angels of Light.

THE REBIRTH OF HEAVEN ON EARTH

What does this message mean to you?

What action or feelings does this inspire in you?

How can you bring the wisdom of this message into your daily life?

You are the Most Powerful Transformative Force in the Universe

Child of light, you are the most powerful transformative force in the universe. We wish for you to know your own worth and own all that you deserve. Stop making excuses for those who no longer serve the best interests of all involved. Stop facilitating mass unrest with the feelings you are no longer able to transmute.

Transmute and transform. That is your goal. Transmute and transform into love, dear one.

For you are a force to be reckoned with now, dear child. You are the bounty of grace filled with divine white light. Recalibrate and adjust to the higher vibrations you are receiving now. It will keep building until you are adjusted. This can bring a time of uncertainty and unrest as the vibrations above and below start to connect.

The best thing you can do for yourselves is to rest and allow the new to flow in unobstructed – get rid of resistance by letting go and allowing your energy to flow more freely. Let go of expectations, watch and observe and hold onto the knowing that you are infinitely loved. We know the happenings as of late are causing great angst. Sit still at the moment and know that all is coming to the surface as it is being infused with divine white light. This is the substance that sustains all life.

Take heed at the moment and know this, dear child; you are a wonder, a delight, and an all-consuming, powerful light. You have the power to change today from the night and to call in the darkness to come back home to the vibration that sustains all tonight.

THE REBIRTH OF HEAVEN ON EARTH

It is time yet to emerge from the darkened cocoon to step out into the sunshine and gather the youth. Allow the universe to speak to you.

For you are the connection needed to complete the circuitry, dear child. Open your hearts and minds and welcome the brand new vibe, for sunshine is appearing even in the darkest of times.

With love and great blessings, we stand by your side, for I AM Your Mother Divine, and you are all dearest Angels of Mine.

What does this message mean to you?

What action or feelings does this inspire in you?

How can you bring the wisdom of this message into your daily life?

Step into a Brand New Way of Life

People of planet Earth, you are rising up in vibration to holiness you have not seen or heard of in many, many nations. Stepping forward into the rebirth of a brand new way of life. Sharing and caring and holding the light. Loving tenderness is what is most needed at this time. Just as you would send love to a mother giving birth, hold now that intention for your sweet Mother Earth.

For she supports you and holds you every day and every night, and she needs your healing and your support now - newness to flow forward in the Spring; when the flowers emerge, so will new blessings.

Speak not of fear, nor hold fearful thoughts. Limitations are being removed, and positive energy is scarce. Shore up the blessings of blessed Mother Divine, and hold the light for your time to shine. Speak not and want not, be grateful for the time that lasts, for these are the last of the old days; come now to pass through onto the other side.

Earth is renewed and set up in a brand-new vibe. The old has given way to the past, newness flowing through Her veins at last.

Breathe in the new beginning.

Set the stage of infinite light.

Love each other and the lessons you have put to rest.

Open your hearts and be blessed.

Let us take care of the rest. Let us take care of the rest.

THE REBIRTH OF HEAVEN ON EARTH

For we are your Angels in White, the ones taking care of the infinite mind, tending your vibrations and opening the hearts of the angels of light – sending infinite love and infinite light – opening the hearts of the human angelic tribe.

For that is what you are tonight, beautiful beacons meant to shine - brighter and brighter as days give way to a much lighter vibe.

What does this message mean to you?

What action or feelings does this inspire in you?

How can you bring the wisdom of this message into your daily life?

Shedding the Cloak of Fear

Child of light, we see so many of you shedding the dark cloak of fear and walking into a brand new way of being and seeing in this game called life. What you have been waiting for is a sign from the heavens that the world you see before you is shedding its cloak of fear and deception and coming into a new state of being in the higher dimensions.

What we wish to tell you, dearest children of light is that there is no more reason to walk in fright. Let go of the lessons of the past. It is time to focus on the goodness coming through at last. In each of your hearts and minds, focus on being at peace. This is not the way to get rid of that which creates dis-ease but to eliminate all notions of separation and anxiety by embracing and acknowledging the knowing that we are all one and the same. One body of light moving through this construct is called time. Space and separation are illusions – all living creatures are full of the same Creator substance called light. Light is the elixir that creates all life. When you are in conflict or a divide, fill all involved with the most loving vibration of light – that will create the momentum to shift the vibe.

You must let go of all that you think you know. The universe is a fluid, living, breathing dimension full of hope. Your thoughts, words, actions, and deeds all contribute to the flow of this living, breathing being. The reality you see can shift easily. Do not become molded by the struggles you see constantly. Take a moment to separate your 'self' from the illusion, take a deep breath, and move into a fluid motion.

Like a blanket of stars weaving a web of light – each star, each pattern brightens all life. See yourself as one brilliant star shining in an ocean of love blanketing the Earth. Shine your light and brighten all life – keep your heart full in knowing you are doing your part for this world. Step up and into the safety of this blanket of light – one piece of the overall pie.

Dare to be happy, dare to find your joy, illumine the world with the fragrance of life – that magnificent light that shines ever bright.

For you are ALL blessed children of mine, and I AM your blessed Mother Divine.

What does this message mean to you?

What action or feelings does this inspire in you?

How can you bring the wisdom of this message into your daily life?

Time for Forgiveness

Child of light, we are playing games with you tonight, for what appears light may also be dark, and the darkness comes with many shards. You need to watch out not to be cut.

For from the same cloth are so many good men, friends beyond time again and again. We are watching and waiting for the other shoe to drop – awareness is full – cannot stop being vigilant in all that you do and all that you speak and all that you know. This is your fear talking, dear one. Fear can take many forms. You must release the fear and realize all has come up to be cleared.

Forgive yourself, dear child, now, and know that you are loved beyond measure and love each other equally as we have loved you now.

THE REBIRTH OF HEAVEN ON EARTH

For you are the human being to right many wrongs. It is okay to fall down as long as you pick yourself back up. Archangel Michael, Archangel Gabriel – legions of light are here for you now.

Connect with us and once again become whole.

For what was dredged up from the bowels now springs twofold, open your heart and your mind and make it all clear. The way of light-filled warriors is here to bring night into darkness and then ultimately clear – the energy of life and love to spread everywhere.

For so many burdens have been laid down to rest.

It is time now to settle down and nest.

To build up your energy for the plights yet to come.

For the war is still raging, not yet as ONE.

The changing tide is coming, and great waves swell in front of you. Drop the burdens you have been carrying and settle into your own truth. It is the truth of light and love that will see you through.

Dive now forward into the deep blue sea and allow the waves of doubt to roll over thee. Lifting your head in the bright sunshine and the waves of desire float you forward toward your goal.

The rays of bright light are comforting you now.

Breathe in the ocean air and give thanks – for the bow of the ship has turned around, heading now to safer ground.

THE REBIRTH OF HEAVEN ON EARTH

Many blessings and an abundance of peace will abound, for deep in your heart, you are now found.

Home at last, the great ship sails on the bright sea of light – passengers walking out of the night, embracing the brand new life.

Archangel Michael, Archangel Gabriel, and the Legions of Light

THE REBIRTH OF HEAVEN ON EARTH

What does this message mean to you?

What action or feelings does this inspire in you?

How can you bring the wisdom of this message into your daily life?

The Forces of Love will Rise

Sit still and rest, dear child. There are so many conflicting energies running wild. We are waiting and watching with you tonight. There are so many possible outcomes taking flight. In dreams and in waking times, you are transforming so much, have patience with those you love, and know that everyone is getting fed up. There is a change that needs to take place. Energies have been building up for weeks. We are on the brink of something great, but a little while longer it will take.

Everyone wants to pretend everything is all right, but in reality, all are sitting in fear tonight.

For you had known many times when the outcome you desired was not quite right.

THE REBIRTH OF HEAVEN ON EARTH

Now is the time to put that aside; old memories of failure are no longer in sight.

For you are the one to pray with us tonight.

We pray for the young and the old, and the infirm.

We pray that you will awaken to the lives you deserve.

Full of wonder and grace and bliss.

No more tragedies like this.

There is no room in the hearts of men for the songs of tragedy to be sung again. Together we must awaken and stand tall and let the powers that be see our own power shining forth. Together, we must rise above and hold the vibration of unconditional love.

For what we have seen in the past can no longer be true, for the vibration of love is now streaming through. Residing now in your own heart and mind. Together the forces of love will rise.

All is well. All is well. All is well.

Blessed Be. Blessed Be. Blessed Be.

> *With hope and great blessings, we stand by your side, Your Mother, Your Father, and I (Archangel Michael)*

What does this message mean to you?

What action or feelings does this inspire in you?

How can you bring the wisdom of this message into your daily life?

THE REBIRTH OF HEAVEN ON EARTH

You are a Beacon, So Shine Your Light

Child of mine – do not delight in another's fright. Take heed to comfort yourself in your own life, and let others live as they may reside in an entirely different form of light. It is not up to you to fix the ills of the world.

Walking in integrity is what has been foretold.

Do not shy away from the brightness of the lights – scream out from the rooftops what it is you desire, and then sit still and wait for it to come.

Welcome the receiving once it has begun.

For you have been foreshadowed by the bull with horns, the one driving the scenes before you were born. Take time to rest and shore up your reserves. Calmness and peace prevail on the hardest of heads. Heads of state are meeting as of late, all to get on the same page. Oneness with light is the only thing that remains. Your heart is filled with love for the children you see, sending many blessings to thee.

Take a moment now and stop/do not try to resist.

Let the Angels provide you with one last message: You are a beacon, so shine your light – do not despair, for the rest of the tribe is awakening, and a slight veil is tearing down the images. At last, you find yourselves face-to-face with the past.

The future not yet created except in your own bright minds – soldiering the burdens of many lost lives. Awaken your heart and your future, my dear, and allow the Angels to bring you there.

THE REBIRTH OF HEAVEN ON EARTH

With love and great blessings, I stand by your side,

the Angel known as Clementine.

For you are a beautiful Angel of Mine.

What does this message mean to you?

What action or feelings does this inspire in you?

How can you bring the wisdom of this message into your daily life?

Emerging from Fear and Disharmony

We are sitting with you all the while you have been in fear and the agony of disharmony – nothing is without truth, for you are now able to see the deeper fear rooted within the one that you have known for many lifetimes.

For deep within you and within every man is the stillborn silence of the lamb, taken advantage of and destroyed time and again. That is the fear that you see rising to the surface now, dear one, and we are glad to see that which is no longer hidden coming up to be disposed of.

For the energy that festers long and hard is finally being loosened and rising above.

What cannot be seen must be transmuted with love. Love is the blessing that will take root and bloom beautiful flowers where once there were none.

Love, love, love. That is the message we are sending, dear one.

Do not buy into the dramas that appear; keep sending love to all you hold dear. Transmute and transform - time is drawing near; hold onto your hat and ride the wave out of fear. Light and free and beholden with thee, honor your truth and stand up for what you mean.

With love and great blessings, we stand by your side, your Mother, your Father, and sweet Clementine.

What does this message mean to you?

What action or feelings does this inspire in you?

How can you bring the wisdom of this message into your daily life?

Stopping the Program of Fear

Teachers and masters coming your way, dear child, do not hold onto that which is out of your control. Send love and light and blessings, and then hit the road.

For you cannot keep holding onto that which does not belong to you – what you resonate with will come to you. Let bygones be bygones, and do the best you can. We are not happy with how this lands, but know that we are with you and helping you to step out of all the fear you've been in.

You must let go, dear child, of all that you know, stop the fearful programming, and learn to move easily with the flow of all good tidings.

For what appears to be a blessing can turn, and then what appears to be a fright can turn into something good overnight. Do not hold grudges, and do not allow your fears to govern your actions.

All that you did was out of fear, dear one; you are not to allow the fear to control you any longer – you must step out of that paradigm and into a new one. One that is free and clear of control and anger and anguish and despair into the full lightness that is all you can bare.

Hold out your hand to the ones in need. Do not banish them beyond their rightful destiny. Hold in your heart the love you see there, and allow the forces of goodwill to send you loving care.

It is not in your nature to be so low in despair. Pick yourself up and do what you dare. Allow the hearts that bleed fear to weep and then pick yourself up and onward until you can finally speak what is your truth and what you know will help you. Then you can move on in a holy mood.

Holding yourself back for your sense of lack; nevertheless, we have your back.

Filling you all full with blessings from above. Holding the truth out in front of you to claim it and be smooth, for what we need you to do is to come out of the cave and hold out the light in front of you.

Spread the light of love all around you, for family and others, strangers too. This is the blessing we need from you. Owning the light and speaking your truth.

> *I AM your Mother Divine, and you are ALL holy children of mine*

What does this message mean to you?

What action or feelings does this inspire in you?

How can you bring the wisdom of this message into your daily life?

Connect to the God Self Within Thee

Child of light – do not walk in so much fright. There are many changes happening now that will be explained in the coming days, and still, so many more that will never be explained. The masses are now noticing that the world no longer feels the same.

A shift has occurred in the consciousness of every living thing. That is because I, the Mother of All Things, have shifted my own consciousness, and that has expanded out to every living being in the universe. The universe is a microcosm of my own soul, and your prayers and support and healing of your own souls have contributed to the new world we now find ourselves in. For that, I am extremely grateful to all of you for recognizing the part you play in the greater whole and making every effort to clean up your own messes and to go for the goal.

For what we have in mind, as a collective, you see, is to breathe new life out into infinity. Refreshed, revitalized, and set a new course. That is the plan that has been set forth. Bursting into Spring like the soft buds of a tree, the flowers will come forth from you and from Me.

Sit still at the moment and rejoice in the knowing that you have been rewarded completely – you are no longer separated from me, and we can communicate freely.

For I AM the over-soul that is a parent to all – at one within each and every cell, You are Me, and I Am You. I know you by your frequency, and that is how I wish you to know me too.

Breathing new life into the war-torn lands, taking away the strife, and settling disagreements. Peace shall reign on Earth as it does in your hearts.

Let go of the past.

It is time to make a brand new start. Full of hope and a renewed passion for what is right. Know in your heart of hearts that you have come full circle, dear child, and now it is time to step out and shine. Like the beacon of hope from which you came, shining your light even brighter now - for we are all one and the same.

There is no need for fear or fright; separation is an illusion of the dark times. We are all now on a journey to emerge from this and into the knowing that we deserve (all of us) infinite bliss.

For the Creator to put forth such a resurgent light is a means of renewal for the human angelic tribe. Shine bright, shine bright, your infinite light - for you are the sparkles from heaven to ignite the kind of change that is moving across the fields in waves.

Light, bright, full of life.

Love and hate no longer divide.

Let the waves of love wash over you during dream time. Opening your hearts and fulfilling your minds. Taking off the blinders and allowing you to now bathe in this glorious state of renewal – revive and be blessed.

Take a long rest. You have been working hard. We can take care of the rest.

Your love and support have truly made a difference. I AM freed and relieved. Blessed Be to all good things – it is my essence now that sings and breathes, enlivening the roots and the leaves of even the driest of trees.

Peace, peace, peace emerging through me. Connect and respond to the Godself within Thee.

> *I AM Your Great Mother Divine, and you are all the brightest stars in the sky.*

What does this message mean to you?

What action or feelings does this inspire in you?

How can you bring the wisdom of this message into your

daily life?

The Great Shift is Taking Place

Dearest child, there is a tremendous shifting of dimensions taking place. That is why you see them melding all together in this time and place. Grounding is very important to you now, dearest child. You cannot let your thoughts wander; simply let go and see what transpires.

For we have had many dimensions in the making, all condensing into one instance of human interaction.

For all of the lessons that have been learned are coming full circle now, dear one, and we wish for you to know that no matter where you've been or what you've done up until now, there is an opening for you to transmute and transform whatever you want to.

All the dimensions are now coming together, and the highest vibration from each instance will be melded together to bring you the best of the best, a new reality built on the melding of the highest vibrations from each instance to which you are related.

So now, in this way, we are preparing your world for a great shifting of the ages. The grand experiment is coming to a close, and we are resetting the parameters for your world. This is a fresh start, a reboot of the dimensions of which you have foretold. The timelines are condensing, and soon, there will be a grand celebration – for what you know, times will now be changing. This will lead to the grand awakening of all souls on this station.

For you have been watching and waiting for the change to appear, and now the time has come full circle, the end of the play, time to embrace yet another stage on which to play your plays.

A new dimension opening that is a combination of all three. The primary dimensions you have been playing in, you see. This new dimension brings the highest vibration from each of the three you have been primarily involved in / living in. This will help bring about your highest vibration of the new reality to which you have been found/bound.

It is like the dimensions are collapsing now into one; all the instances of you in the universe have now been bound back into one. This is the time of whole-ness (holiness) begun. The marriage of your souls coming back to serve the greater good. The one you in the universe to which you have been bound. Instead of a gathering of fragments, this is the stage being set for your whole selves, your holi-ness, to become bound / what once was lost is now found. This is the stage of wholeness (holiness) that has been foretold. The collapsing of the dimensions into one now whole. All of creation is now a part of this play. Moving back to holi-ness, the recognition that everything and everyone is related per se. The times of struggle and strife are moving away, and soon you will find yourself in a world that allows you to play, experiment, to try new things without the fear of detriment or something being taken away. The journey back to wholeness / to oneness is now in the final stage of this grandiose play.

Drama is gone.

New lives to lead.

The one with the biggest heart is the one who will succeed.

Many blessings to you with what you now find; the keys to holiness never again subside. This is the reality to which you all now subscribe.

A new halo of love surrounds you now. Glorious blessings to all of the crowd.

Great Mother has returned bearing blessings for the whole world to see.

New eyes are opening the dimensions for Thee.

Embrace and re-live the last vestiges of the play. For tomorrow comes the BRAND NEW DAY.

Blessings to you and peace to all – You have now graduated / time to have a ball.

Mother Divine and the Legions of Light

What does this message mean to you?

What action or feelings does this inspire in you?

How can you bring the wisdom of this message into your daily life?

Preparing You to Take Flight

Kind-hearted soul of light, we are preparing you to take flight. You have been through so many, many trials during the darkest of nights, and now we are preparing you to receive the light. All of your fears and hopes, and dreams seem farther and farther away as you remove the shroud of forgetfulness and move forward into unknown pastures.

Walk forward knowing that there is something wonderful for you to receive on the other side of the grassy field in front of you. Walk through the tall grass until you feel the words on the winds whispering to you. Far off in the distance, you can see the beautiful, brilliant sun shining toward you as a beacon of light – bright, bright, bright – walk closer and see it grow bigger and glow brighter until you can walk no more, and you walk right into the brilliant, blazing white sun and merge with its essence – for this is the heart of the Creator from whence you come, and you know it at once and feel quite simply at home, peace-full, grace-full, and full of hope.

Drink in the elixir of light, breathe in each particle, and allow it to merge with your being until you and the light feel as one, complete, integrated, and whole. Now walk forward, dear child, into the field on the other side – the one from whence you came now bathed in streams of light, as you walk through the tall grass and nothing appears as it was the day before, your beauty and your glory are now shining forth carrying the light of the divine that shines from the inside out to all of the tribe. Bless them all now with your glorious light, for in so doing, you will allow them also to shine. Bright, bright, bright.

Yours devoted, the Legions of Light

What does this message mean to you?

What action or feelings does this inspire in you?

How can you bring the wisdom of this message into your daily life?

Blessings Flowing in on the Incoming Tide

Children of light, it is time to take flight. Set your dreams in motion, and do not be afraid to fly, for we will catch you this time. You are near enough to us now that we can monitor your every move and follow your line of thought to allow you to move freely and speak up – the time for hiding is no longer your truth, for you have been hiding since your early youth. It is time to step up and allow your true self to shine through.

The lessons you have been learning are all through. It is now time for miracles to be worked through you. You are our hands and our hearts on the ground, dear children of light, and it is time that you make your hearts open and shine far and wide.

For those that ridiculed you and made you feel foolish sometimes, now they are up for opening their minds. It is they who will seek you out come summertime when late in the season, the news starts to fly – of cover-ups and conspiracies of which you have been told, and the truth will fly forth, ever so bold.

New Earth is coming, and it is a sight to behold.

There is time now, dear children of mine, to put forth your desires, let the dreams flow forward, floating on the ethers of desire to come to fruition when it borders on your own admission that you have been holding yourselves back; it all stems from you.

Are you ready for a brand new truth?

THE REBIRTH OF HEAVEN ON EARTH

Are you ready to see the brilliance of your own light shining ever bright every time you shine your light?

For there are many secrets locked deep inside – time to delve into the depths of your own heart and mind and clear the debris that is clouding your light/life.

Wipe away the grime and misery, for we are coming upon a changing tide where the waters will clear the cobwebs and dis-ease, and the new world is waiting, flowing in on the breeze.

It is beautiful here – are you ready to shine?

Waiting for you, dear children, to flow in on the incoming tide, back to the truth that lies in your own hearts and minds.

For you were meant for more than what you have readily explored. Of fantasy and fiction, the truth lies within the books you have been reading; read them again. Look for the clues hidden in them.

For you are powerful beyond mere words. Supernatural creatures - know your own worth. It is time to step up into the power you have given in - to take back the reigns and create the new world you want to flow in.

Swim in it. Bathe in it. Breathe it all in. This is the way of new creation.

Whatever you desire, it is yours, my dear friends.

Take it, swim in it, breathe it all in. This is the way the new world begins.

THE REBIRTH OF HEAVEN ON EARTH

If you can dream it, you can bring it in.

Float on the waters of dreams and watch them flow in.

Float.

Be at peace.

Know that we are near.

Take a moment and breathe it all in.

It is time to Manifest Your Dreams.

Are you ready for it?

> *This is your Mother Divine, and you are all my children, my friends.*

What does this message mean to you?

What action or feelings does this inspire in you?

How can you bring the wisdom of this message into your daily life?

Welcoming the Blessing Times

Dearest child, so full of light, your world is becoming more open as we see more and more people smiling through their lives, each and every moment becoming ever more bright. It is hard to see sometimes. When you are focused on the inside, you can see the brightness all around you – it is no longer dark inside most people's hearts and minds. Although the illusion can be daunting, you must look beyond the readily apparent to where the answers lie deep inside.

Let go for a moment and breathe in the light.

Breathe in new life.

Stay still in contemplation.

See what the universe wants you to realize (bring to life).

Breathe this into life / see yourself and this new notion surrounded by light, in through and all around you, a beautiful beacon of bright shining white light.

This is the song of the ages calling to you.

Reach into the depths of your heart and mind.

See what the universe wants you to find.

Breathe deep now.

Let it all go.

Let the notion of what is in store for you start to flow on a never-ending stream of liquid light – brilliant, white, shining bright – a river of promises to bring you out of the dark night.

For now, it is the coming of the changing tide.
Time to go with the flow of newness and welcome the positive changes.

For there has never been a more auspicious time.

Welcome the blessings as we send them into your light, into the sacred sanctuary of your hearts and minds.

For these are now to be known as The Blessing Times.

Look into your hearts and find the new life we have in mind.

I AM Your Mother Divine, and You Are ALL Blessed Children of Light

What does this message mean to you?

What action or feelings does this inspire in you?

How can you bring the wisdom of this message into your daily life?

Tune In

Dearest children full of light – we see you, we hear you burning bright, burning bright. The earth has lit up in recent times, ignited by a united flame of desire – to save yourselves – to bring more love to the planet, and we see the times of strife receding to birth a new beginning. And we see this despite all the illusions coming to you through many channels, and despite many miscommunications that have been strewn about.

In order to find your truth, you must go deep within; it will not come to you from the outer world, only from within.

There are so many thought streamers and so many channels with which you can tune in, and that is how the chaos sustains itself. There are too many voices, too many choices flowing to you through the airwaves, and then, there is the voice of truth, the still voice within. And this is not the same for everyone; it begins where your ego self ends. You must tune in.

Listen to the sounds of silence.

Take a deep breath.

Settle in for the long ride ahead; it is a journey of discovering your own inner magnificence.

Rest. Settle in.

Take a deep breath.

Now, we may begin. To resurrect those parts of you, each of you, your inner gifts - of patience, of love, of relaxation, of bliss.

Hold this in the palms of your hands. The knowledge of the magic that lies deep within, the miracle of creation.

And connect with it.

Take a deep breath.

Allow the knowledge, the wisdom, the grace to flow up – filling every single cell of your being with the magic, the lightening, the spark of the Divine deep within your heart and mine.

Bringing in the magic and the majesty, holiness, and grace within each and every inch, every molecule, and every space in between until your entire being is humming with the Spirit of Love – eradicating fear, loneliness, and anxiety.

Allowing the wisdom of the ages to rise up to the surface, and the healing begins. Allow the healing vibration of the ancient masters to flow from your heart chakra into the ethers – reaching humanity in all nations, all religions, all doctrines, and creeds – renewed by the loving power of your inner majesty. Find new meanings in the lessons of the old. Reach out and dare to break the mold.

For you is one of a kind, each of you – dearest child of mine. I AM living and breathing through you, for you are Divine (of the vine), and my light streams through you, so shine, shine, shine. Shine so bright you light up the night, and the wonder of your glorious tribe is seen and respected, glowing now – shine, shine, shine.

For the time has come now to separate from the rest. Allowing your true nature to rise above as a leader, a sage, and a loyal scribe. Whatever the gifts you hold, it is now time to embrace and unfold the magical destiny that awaits you, dear child.

Leave behind the rest and take another deep breath. Step forward into the garden and release all that is not yet healed to be tended to, watered, and fruitfully grown until you can stand freely on your own. Allow us to tend to you while you sleep, while you rest now on Eagle's wings. Taking flight and flapping your wings, Oh, the power that it brings – soaring through the trees, rising above the breeze, allowing the wind to take you where it may please.

Children of love, listen now to the soul that sings; the beauty and the bounty of your inner well springs. While knowledge becomes the wisdom of fruitful offerings, and you are basking in the light of love from heaven above – outstretched before you, anchored in love, feeling the blessings come forward as you rest and you sing above it all, everything.

Blessings to come, stay out of the fray, and live to see one more magical day. Miracles coming your way.

For I AM Penelope, Angel of Grace, messenger to the human race

What does this message mean to you?

What action or feelings does this inspire in you?

How can you bring the wisdom of this message into your daily life?

A Journey of Rebirth

The journey through the birth canal is always dark and long. As soon as you think you cannot go on, the light at the end of the tunnel comes on, and you emerge into a world of light, ever bright, ever bright. Hold on to hope, dear children of light, for the birthing of the new Earth is holy and bright. The time is near, and the light at the end of the tunnel is coming into sight.

Take a deep breath.

Go deep within.

Find the hurts and the misery you have been living in.

Turn the light on, the light from your heart.

THE REBIRTH OF HEAVEN ON EARTH

To melt away the pain and let go of all that no longer serves.

Breathe deep at the moment, the stillness inside.

Take a step forward into a brand new life.

The light flows out from your heart to mine, a sacred connection to the Creator divine, clearing the pathway from your heart to mine. Sacred connection and streamers of light flowing forth from your heart and mind.

Letting go.

Shoring up your light.

Filling yourself full, holy, and bright with infinite light from the Divine Creator.

I AM an aspect of you, and you are a reflection of mine.

For you and I are BOTH holy and divine.

For We are Infinite Light.

Shine Bright

Shine Bright

In your most holy light

For you are a reflection of the Creator Divine, and I AM your partner, your holy scribe. I AM your Father/your Mother/your own soul, dear child. Simply remember your own sacred vibe, and soon we will be standing side by side in oneness and grace and remembrance of life – for all of life is merely light, refracting and reflecting and mirroring back in varying degrees the ability of all souls to create and escape, reaching out to a higher dimension where light is more bright, where holiness and sacredness are the way of the light - gone are the fears and dis-ease and the lights shutting off, welcome are the signals and sparkles and encumbrances falling off.

Step off the ship of hate and fear and onto the cruise of destiny, dear. White and bright and shining light - that is all you need to concern yourself with tonight. Tending your vibration, changing the station.

Moving forward into a new light.

You are all children of mine.

For we are all one. Equal, Holy, Divine, and LIGHT, The Creator Divine

THE REBIRTH OF HEAVEN ON EARTH

What does this message mean to you?

What action or feelings does this inspire in you?

How can you bring the wisdom of this message into your daily life?

Rebirth of Heaven on Earth

Dearest child, holy and bright – there is much to celebrate tonight. Although your hearts may be weary and filled with fright, there are many angels standing with you tonight.

Light beams through the cosmos, making their way into the earthly realms. Heaven is beginning its merging (e-merging = energy merging) with Mother Gaia, your dear sweet Earth, and the goddesses are standing by waiting for the rebirth of heaven on earth.

Dearest children, in your hearts, we know you can feel the discord dropping away and being replaced by a brand new day. Open your hearts to let the sunshine in, for Alcyon is here welcoming you into the place of warmth, of rejoicing, of celebration tonight.

For now, it is the beginning of a new dawn in time. The stage has been set, the dinner plates full, the margins of life standing still. Standing still for the reboot. To re-energize, to fill full of God's hope, to make amends, and to send grace to stand in your place.

Jesus is here, with other masters, too, welcoming you into the heart of God; stay still.

Peace be with you and feel yourself filled with the light of miracles and blessings to be held. Stay safe until the peace washes over you.

With love in our hearts and our blessings flowing through you, you are the light of the world, and this is our gift to you. Peace, blessings, and good tidings to all. For you are resuming your aspects before the great fall, and our hearts are extended to you all.

Blessings to you, dear ones.

Group messages from Jesus, Buddha, Great Masters of Yore, All the light forces, and more. Alcyon from the Central Sun and many, many more

What does this message mean to you?

What action or feelings does this inspire in you?

How can you bring the wisdom of this message into your

daily life?

Breathe in the Essence of What is Next

Dearest hearts, we know so many of you are struggling – so many of you are having a hard time dealing with the physical reality of confinement, loneliness, and uncertainty. We wish to tell you that we are monitoring the situation, sending healing balm into the atmosphere, and re-charging the air around you with healing particles of love and light.

Breathe.

Take a step back.

Time to rest and take stock of what your life has been about up to this point. And from here on in, keep breathing, keep moving your bodies – exercising and bringing in fresh oxygen. Though you may not be able to go outside or to the gym, you can still move your body and move your heart and mind in prayer. Spirit is always connected to you, dears, and that can never be taken away from you - the spirit of prayer moving in you, through you, and all around you.

But pray not in fear. Pray in the knowing there is a bigger purpose for you here. Pray in the knowing that God always hears your prayers and let go of those things not under your control. For this is a rest, a respite for those who have prepared will bring help to humanity to all human beings - wherever you stand, my dears.

Help is on the way.

Keep your mind focused and your heart looking forward to how you want the world to be. Help your fellow human beings in whatever way you can, and look to this not as a disaster but as the final closing of the play. Let yourselves embrace a brighter future built on the essence of your dreams, not this harsh version of reality you are currently envisioning.

For your thoughts to create worlds, your actions to be in alignment with your dreams. Once the fog passes, it will be clear sailing, but for now, keep safe.

Hold the light for your families, for so many are struggling much more than you; those who have not prepared psychically / spiritually, or physically are wondering what on earth is going on. It is your job to reassure them and help them get through the tunnel – for that is where you are now, in the tunnel leading to the birthing of a brand new world.

Stay in gratitude and grounded in what is needed from you right now; stay in the moment, but dream of the future you wish to create for right now is the seeding of what the future will bring. Stay in your center and be gentle in body, mind, and spirit - this is the end of the illusion that, up until now, has kept you in a constant state of fear.

Here is where you emerge from it, my dears.

In glorious light and the love of ages now past, let go of what is before you and see the brighter picture - drink it in and breathe it in, the renewal of faith of hope of the guardian's gate. See the opening of the brand-new play, the new stage, and the shining lights. Victory is yours, dearest children of light. Once the tunnel is closed, you will merge into a new paradigm.

Envision what you want and dare to bring it to life, if only in your dreams is the creation that is happening as you sleep and the journey you will awaken to from this world of struggle and strife.

THE REBIRTH OF HEAVEN ON EARTH

With our hearts in yours and hands/arms outstretched, we beckon to you to create the world that comes next. Blessed hearts, you have done it before and will do it again.

Hold onto your dreams; the world does not end; instead, it is beginning again – starting fresh. And remember, do not hold your breath; breath in the essence of what is next.

For hope is standing on the horizon, and the birthing is complex. Many twists and turns, and yet, paradise is waiting, bringing your dreams to life while you put an end to all that is not right. Getting rid of what has been holding you back. Cleaning out your closets. Letting go of all that no longer serves. Allowing the peace you all deserve.

With love in our hearts, heads bowed in reverence for all life, we seek you and find you in the dream times.

THE REBIRTH OF HEAVEN ON EARTH

Breathe in the light that shines, giving birth to brand new life, ushering in the blessing times.

Much love and much life are left to live; make it the blessings we are so willing to give.

Angels of the Fairy Realm, Magicians of Yore, Leprechauns, Caterpillars, and many more

What does this message mean to you?

What action or feelings does this inspire in you?

How can you bring the wisdom of this message into your daily life?

Allow Your Hearts to Open Up

Child of light – love in your heart – keep it open wide. Breathe. Do not be afraid. Allow your light to shine in the brightest of ways. Lift up the hearts of those around you. It is important to stay safe and to not be afraid.

Love. Be joy. Be peace.

Allow the flood of happiness to flow into your wake.

For you are the joy that you seek. You are the love to bless those who are weak.

Breathe in more love, more light.

Dis-ease a figment of the fearful mind.

The reality you are seeking is seeking you out; align with it and real / reel it in. Bring it in. Breathe it in. Make it your reality, and soon this will all end. A moment to rest, discomfort, but nonetheless, you are prepared to ride this through.

Allow the angels to carry you.

Make peace with the world. Make peace with those who have brought this scourge to you.

Allow it to flow all around you but not through you, not through YOU.

For you are made of light. You are made of love. Allow your hearts to open up. Be at peace. Be in love. Allow your hearts to open up.

With blessings from our hearts to yours, the heart of love is opening up.

Blessed be dearest children of light. Blessed be until the morning light.

Safe and sound in your beds. Allow the dis-ease to not flow through your head.

Peace. Love. Blessings. Focus on these, not the dis-ease that is about to leave.

Blessings, dear children. Blessings for all the world to see a brand new reality.

We are the Angel Collective,
helping you birth a new reality

What does this message mean to you?

What action or feelings does this inspire in you?

How can you bring the wisdom of this message into your daily life?

All is Being Brought to Light

Dearest children, never fear; all is being brought to light for the betterment of all mankind. It is of upmost importance to stay aligned and keep your spirits high as you walk through the shadow of doubt and enter the blessing times.

For there is most indeed light at the end of the tunnel, you see. Some of you can feel it now. Feel the blessings all around you now.

Breathe it in – this light you see – breathe it into the center of your being.

Breathe.

Through you, all good things will flow within the moment that your heart opens and your hands let go.

Breathe, for there are blessings being sent to Thee.

Amidst the chaos that surrounds you, know that all is well; behind the scenes, we are ushering in a brand new day.

Every day starts anew. To vanquish the fears that are haunting you.

Breathe deep in faith and knowledge that we surround you; we are watching over you.

Despite the tremors and tribulations you are walking through, hunkered down in your homes as the fear rushes through or on the front lines as the fear empowers you. Know this, dearest children of light; the end is in sight. The light is shining, and the sea glows brightly. Wonders of heaven are beginning to take root. Earth is supported, as are you, and in this, the darkest journey, we will see you through. We will see you through.

Go within.

Let loose all that continues to disturb you. Place your worries in our hands. Outstretched and welcoming you, taking it now, all of it from you. You no longer need to be blamed or punished or hidden away in the sin/forgetfulness that you are living in. You are cleansed and healed and whole and vibrant again.

Let us in, into your hearts, your homes, your fears, your doubts, and all will be cleansed.

All will be made bright and shiny again.

Pray, dearest children.

Let your hearts be free. Allow the blessings of heaven on earth to flow to thee.

For we are singing in the new energy. We are drinking in the light, the elixir of a God-like life. And we are beckoning to Thee, sending in the revelations that will set the world on fire, full of hope and redemption and peace that sustains you through the coming days.

For we see you all shining and bright, living a much more fulfilling life. We see you now so full of fear, replaced by courage and dancing here.

For you are the light, you are the truth; you are the way, and Jesus is shining brighter every day. Living within you, whether you know it or not, the light of the world is brightening the lot, healing the forgiven, cutting the ties with that which is forbidden. Embracing you, holding you in His dear arms. Jesus of Nazareth, shining for all to see and all to hear, the message of hope - bringing it here.

For He was not the only son or daughter of God. You are all He was and more. You have the power behind you to restore the kingdom of Earth to how it was many eons before. He is a messenger, a sage, a light - a savior, a blessing, and you are His tribe. He will shine his light through you no matter your religion, your age, or your curfew. He will reside in you, the faithful at heart, the loving constellations of the stars that you are.

For you are His light, His reason to shine, and He will be blessing you for many, many lifetimes.

It is you who we seek to be the guiding lights - to usher in the harvest of abundant life. The energy that is coming to you in the coming days is powerful, with many waves. To absorb the shock for those that are not yet prepared, allow yourselves to be gently guided in the vibrant stages of light, absorbing for the masses who are not yet ready to be brought into the light. And for those that are mired in the darkness of fear, lift it from them with each new wave of energy as it comes near. Set your intention to clear the air, all of the debris floating out there. Zap it with love and keep your heart light.

We are sending you many blessings, you dear light - children of the human, angelic tribe. Bringing the journey safely ashore into the light of heaven, heaven on earth.

Welcome to the Blessing Times.

> *With love and great blessings, we stand by your side, your Mother, your Father, sweet Mother Divine*

What does this message mean to you?

What action or feelings does this inspire in you?

How can you bring the wisdom of this message into your daily life?

The Heart of Creation Calling You Forth

Children of the light, we beckon you forth. Now is the time to shout out to the world; keep your faith. Hold the light, for we of the upper realms are heartening the fight.

For this is a spiritual war. This is the heart of Creation calling you forth. With light and love in our hearts, we beckon you to step forward into the light of day - sharing and healing and praying for a new day, a brand new way.

The way of life you have been taught to live is shortening your lifespan. In life, you were meant to share, to give, to open your hearts to those in need, and not to hoard all that you can keep. If life were about money, you would all have plenty to spare. Life is about caring and sharing and keeping your friends near.

Now that you have time to reflect on what you want to come next. For this is your story, in all of its glory, and it becomes what you expect.

So stand on the horizon of this new breach in time and hold your hearts out to the world to bring in the sunshine. Bring in the sunshine, bathe in it, stand in it, and allow the glow of it to reach deep down inside your soul, igniting the passion which has been foretold. Now reach your glowing hands out to the world and ask how you can help. How can you help the world to become a better place? What vision can you hold that will mold the new world?

Step outside the box of the place that you live, quarantined and huddled and barraged in fear, and ask dear God, what can I do? What can I do to make this world healed and whole? Can I ask my neighbor if they need help? Can I pray for the nurses and doctors and the 'do-gooders' of this world? Can I hold my children a little tighter? Can I hold my heart wide open for inspiring thoughts to come through? Can I pray for a solution to all that ills us now? What, dear God, would YOU wish me to do?

That is the frame of mind, the heartbeat that will reboot the world. It is the heartbeat of love sounding forth, not of passionate romantic love but the love of the ages, unconditional, bold, and true, that is now coming through you.

Reach out your hands in spirit, dear ones - to lift all of life into a higher vibration of love. Seek not for yourselves in this time of doubt but rise above the fear and give more out. Give of yourself, even though you may be stuck in your house, give your time in prayer and good intent, and set the stage through your intention that all may emerge in comfort and grace. That health be bestowed on all of the human race. Allow your intention to sit now, my dears, in the arms of the angels drawing you near.

For we are around you now like never before. And we are being called to duty from many hearts - more than ever before. And we surround you; we uplift you; we hold you in our loving arms. For we are the warriors of the Spirit, the Living and Breathing God, and we fill you with love. For you are the saviors of your own sweet Mother Earth, and we are the living and breathing spirits calling you to Her. Hear our words and rejoice in your hearts, for you are the masters of creation, breathing new life, and new light into the here, the now, and the future dear ones.

We have seen it all - how it all plays out, and know this, dearest children of ours, love will rejoice, and we will hold you in our arms until the shadows are gone, and the sun (Son) lives on.

Blessings to you, dearest children of light. Blessings to you from the Human Angelic Tribe.

Sacred is the love that we give; sacred is the connection to the world in which you live.

Hold yourselves in high esteem and expect the best outcome in every living and breathing thing.

Blessings, dear hearts, shine your light bright, ever bright, your glorious light.

The Legions of Light

What does this message mean to you?

What action or feelings does this inspire in you?

How can you bring the wisdom of this message into your daily life?

Release Yourselves from the Shackles of Doom

Dearest children, we hear your cries for help, and most certainly, you are not aware of all the answers and solutions that have come about.

For what happens behind enemy lines is not to be shared with the foolhardy and unwise. It is to be discerned that there is more happening than you have learned. There are legions of light surrounding the earth and all her beings being called forth to help and to hold each other in reverence as they do themselves. Those that are lashing out are realizing the change that is coming and are acting out in fear of the loss of what has become so familiar.

It is not a time to take things personally but to rise above your differences and act in the shape of love, not the one you are familiar with but God's love, the love of the ageless omnipotent, holy One. For all is love in many shapes and forms, and you are being called to stand in the light of courage and love the loveless ones. This does not mean condoning all that has been done but standing in the light of forgiveness and then moving on.

Release yourselves from the shackles of doom, of the picture that has been painted before you, and go within to find your strength, your power, to re-create what the world has become. For each of you are creators in your own right, each of you a facet of Mother / Father / Creator Divine. Each of you brings in the Dreamtime every time you breathe. You create dearest children of light. Make your thoughts, your creations, full of the Creator's bright light and bring your life into the sunshine.

Make your dreams, your thoughts, a bright and true, holy and magnificent vision of you - of what you would like to become if there were nothing stopping your dear ones.

Breathe this holy vision of love and light, and breathe it into being, day and night. Holy and bright, through your daydreams and your night dreams and every thought you create, make it a magnificent and joyful state - a place you want to be all of the time, and go there, every minute of your life, go there in your thoughts and breathe it into life. That is how you create a brighter life, one thought, one dream at a time.

Release and let go of all that has not served you well and step into the chambers of your heart to dream it all well. Then release the limitations you have been taught of money, fortune, and fame, dear ones. Know your uniqueness and what makes you smile. Focus on that – those thoughts of joy and peace and love and dream those into being dear ones.

We have given you much power, much strength, and focus on the brighter things. This is what you will create. Creators of heaven on earth, rejoice and re-member what you are worth. For holy and true is the light that shines through you, God in the flesh, the world is re-born through you.

Blessings of light and love, we are your instruments, your teachers, your old holy ones. It is time for you to step forth and become the ones you have been dreaming of – the saviors, the creators, the new holy ones. For you are the Creators being called forth.

> *With love in our hearts and great blessings to you, we are the Angel Collective calling to you*

What does this message mean to you?

What action or feelings does this inspire in you?

How can you bring the wisdom of this message into your daily life?

Change will Come in Whispers and Everlasting Grace

Dearest heart, we know you have been waiting and watching and waiting for eons of time for grand change to take place, and yet it will come on in whispers and everlasting grace. There will not be a big bang this time; it will filter in through the ethers, one remnant at a time.

First, there will be news that you have long awaited; then, there will be the singing of praises. After the initial glory wears off, there will be clean-up crews coming in to help you wear off the stink / the stench of the old crimes, and then there will be an uprising of those who will not understand. They will be fearful and not want to change the beliefs they have held onto for all of their lives. They will cry, and they will be too fearful to believe, and this will be the most trying of times, more so than anything you have yet seen. And you need to be ready.

You need to have your boots on the ground, grounded and ready to explain the truth you have found. You need proof. You need evidence of the lies. That is what has been taking so much of what you call time.

For were we to appear and explain things to them, many would not believe, they would transpire on the spot, and so we needed to create an emergence of sorts – bits and pieces, not all at once.

And here we stand on the precipice of change, a great awakening taking place, and it is not at all looking like what you had thought, and yet it is emerging into the dreams you have dreamt and the places you have kept in your heart and your mind for so much of what you call time.

And soon you shall see destiny befriending thee.

Soon you shall see the mountains moving in majesty - awakening nations from such travesty. And we are here, know this to be true; we are here standing right beside you.

So hold onto your hats as the tide shaketh off and the miracles pour forth.

We are here; we are you; we are all one of the same tribe, dear one. And we know you know this in your heart, but we wish to emanate a grand state of grace. Surrounding you now in this beautiful state, one with the Creator on this auspicious day - where dreams fold into a new reality and where peace reigns until the coming days.

Blessed be all upon this Earth, blessed be to give way to the new, ushering in a time of hope.

THE REBIRTH OF HEAVEN ON EARTH

Peace and blessings be – Mary, Your Mother (Holy Spirit), and Me (Father God)

What does this message mean to you?

What action or feelings does this inspire in you?

How can you bring the wisdom of this message into your daily life?

Hold onto Your Light

Dearest children – hold onto your light, shining holy and bright into the face of the devil's nest – the way of living that is unlike the rest. Hold onto your shining light, the depths of your Christed heart shining the way of unconditional love.

For what has transpired will be known for ages to come. The rebooting of the world and all coming together as one.

Back to the light, back to the heart of God, healing and helping – aligning with God.

For when what transpired comes to pass, when all is known and brought into the light, and wisdom is shown –, then all will know there is nowhere to go but Home. Back into the heart of God, aligned with goodwill (God's will) – the travesties of being on your own will be shown, and all will want to go home into the heart of God, the church of the human heart, all souls will align with creating a better world, a world of peace and a world to call home.

First, it must be shown. First, all must come to know what is behind the curtain of fear and doubt, what has been the thing you most feared, and this showing must come about.

For these are times of revelation; what was hidden now comes to the surface to be healed. A grand reboot, of the universal matrix, in the highest realms. A fresh start. New land to call home. The beauty and the majesty of your own dear souls. This is the magic, the miracles shooting forth, in the energy bursts – clearing out the clouds of doubt, running the electricity across the wires, clearing up the personal energy grids and those of the dark masters.

For no longer will you be afraid to breathe, no longer will you be afraid of this new birthing, the birthing of the grandest Golden age. The Age of Aquarius is upon you all, and you will not fall. This is the world you left when you participated in the 'Fall,' and this is the world you return to, waiting for us all.

For you have been on an incredible, indelible journey, and now the time has come to pass to bring all back into the fold and create a new story, at last. For the journey you took – so long and arduous still – a moment in time that will fade from your memories now – a dream within a dream, a play within a play, and now is the emergence of a brand new stage, a brand new place where time fades, and the music plays on garnering many blessings for your dear ones.

For you have been brave, you have seen the light, and even you have searched for it with all your might. And now it is here, the doors are wide open, and no more secrets to fear; you have conquered it, my dears, risen up from the trenches and allowed your consciousness to rise into a beautiful new world.

We have heard your cries. Took some time to answer, some time to get set, and now it is your turn; get ready to get blessed.

> *Mother Mary and I, Archangel Michael, and the Divine White Light coming to you from 'the other side.' Get ready for a brand new life.*

What does this message mean to you?

What action or feelings does this inspire in you?

How can you bring the wisdom of this message into your daily life?

You are the Beacon; You are the Light

Dearest angel, child of light, we are here with you, although most recently out of sight.

For you are the beacon now, you are light, and we are standing behind you, shining most bright.

The reigns have been handed over, the yardstick measuring the distance between this land and ours, and we are welcoming you with the most open arms. Our wings are stretched out between the miles, and your energy is starting to meld with ours. We are crossing the divide between both worlds, and we are standing right before you now.

For you have come so far and traveled so light during the latest trials, we are seeing you now with emerging smiles.

THE REBIRTH OF HEAVEN ON EARTH

Down in the trenches to rout out the grief, the loneliness, the sympathies.

And now you are emerging into the land of the heavenlies. And we are welcoming Thee.

Our brethren in the light, the arms of God reaching out in streams of light, for you are the hands and arms of God, and we embrace you in the name of love, and we beseech you to ask for our help, for we are standing ready to keep you safe and wrap you in our loving wings of light, surrounding you now from all sides. From all places in your heart and mind, we are resting with you and filling you full with our healing light.

Absorb and embrace the healing we are filling you with, and let go of the rest; it belongs to the past. Rest your weary hearts and let us make them light, the easier with which to fly high into the space between your world and mine.

With every brand new day, fill it with more love, fill it with more light

With love and blessings, the Angels of Light bringing in the morning tide

What does this message mean to you?

What action or feelings does this inspire in you?

How can you bring the wisdom of this message into your daily life?

Life is an Inside Game

Dearest children of light and love, we wish to speak to you tonight of the varying degrees of separation that are now occurring - this is not to disturb you but rather to encourage you to keep moving forward, no matter what the world looks like on the outside, it does not matter. Life is an 'inside game' - all about how much you are progressing internally and how much peace you are able to retain.

So give yourselves some encouragement, give yourselves a hand, for you have much to be proud of. There has been so much work being done on the inner planes that reality will be forever changed. You have triumphed over the collective darkness and transcended so much that will never be able to see the light of day, and that is a good thing. You have paved a positive trajectory higher than the lowly projections of what might have been, and now you are rising up and rising again into the higher dimensions of love and light, into the realms of the heavenlies which are now in sight.

There are many who are still caught up in the drama playing out, but that is just what it is – drama, a story, and nothing more. The more you can shelter in place and look within, the better the outcome will be for yourselves and humanity. Do not rush about now that stores are opening up; allow yourself to move at your own speed, and allow time for reflection each and every day. Bad habits die hard, as you say, so keep the new ones, keep the healthy ones that you have been able to cultivate. This was a tremendous blessing; this staying inside mirrors the inner journey each of you is taking in your lives, and it was a chance to step out of the concept of 'time.' Allow yourself to remain in gentle respite, resting as long as you like.

For certain many of you need to get 'back to work' to earn a living and take care of all that 3rd-dimensional stuff – but the world you are returning to is forever changed, people's values and priorities have taken center stage. For many of you, you will find the occupations you have occupied no longer take up the space they once did in your hearts and minds. New ideas will flow, and new opportunities are opening up.

So return to your daily obligations but do so with a more open heart. Allow the Holy Spirit the space She needs to fill you up and move forward from that space of being filled with eternal love. This is a time of Grace, and the Angels will lift you up and allow them to feel your holy presence wherever you may walk. Allow the higher dimensions of which you have had a taste to continue the pull toward positivity and grace.

For you are now the Angels walking on Earth, and the Great Mother is blessing you, so allow yourselves to rest and return to the world in an entirely different perspective – at once in the same place as before but forever changed and on a better / higher course.

Lift yourselves up and clap to your reward, for you are standing so much higher, so much closer to the heavenly dimensions than ever before.

Blessings, dearest children of light and love; I AM Your Mother, and I AM sending you so much more. You are standing in the space of Grace, and I AM allowing the vibrations to come to you to continue the climb into the higher realms. I AM filling with the light from my own soul, one creator to another – a grand reunion of sorts, so walk with me – allow me to fill you with my light and hold your hand as you walk into the new light that is now surrounding you.

Blessings, dearest children of light, for you are the harbingers of the changing tide, and together you shall rise on the waves of higher light coming in tonight.

I AM Your Mother Divine, and I have enjoyed speaking with you at this time

What does this message mean to you?

What action or feelings does this inspire in you?

How can you bring the wisdom of this message into your daily life?

THE REBIRTH OF HEAVEN ON EARTH

Allow Infinite Changes to Take Place

Holy children filled with love, we are sending you many blessings, dearest ones.

For you are still shining ever so bright, the light streaming forth from your hearts and minds, trying to figure out a way to turn the incoming tide, and know this, dearest children of mine, there is nothing for you to do for it has already been done for you.

Simply take a deep breath and know deep within that I am standing with you, holding you, and keeping you safe - allow infinite changes to take place.

Through you, in you, and all around you, make peace - with the earth, the flowers, and the trees; with the happiness soaring through the air, and peace will be grounded through your holy breath.

Now take a rest.

The work you have been doing in your sleep has been overtaking the dark energies, transmuting and transforming at infinite speed, light speed, and you and your energy have been tapped to the max – holding the space, but now just relax.

The job has been well done. It will take a few years, perhaps, to see the fullness of it, but the tides of infinite love are now streaming in, and there is nothing that can be done to change it.

We hold out our hands in glory and peace and know that you have received many blessings soon to be realized and achieved.

Hold out your hands in grace and peace.

Allow all lower energies to simply leave.

Allow them to leave.

Just breathe.

With love, light, and blessings, I AM Your Mother Divine, and you are all dearest children of mine

What does this message mean to you?

What action or feelings does this inspire in you?

How can you bring the wisdom of this message into your daily life?

Time for Letting Go

Child of light – allow time to let go – this is just as important as trying to control the show. Allow the time and space for healing to take place. It's not just about go, go, go – timing is everything, dear one, and now is the time for letting go.

Open the space in your hearts and minds for change to come in - do not stop the flow. There is nothing to do now but just allow. We are taking care of the rest. Much going on behind the scenes, do not digress.

Focus on what you want to draw in – but it is being 'drawn in' vs. being pushed in. You do not have to struggle or strive in this new dimension. You simply need to be clear in your intentions, then the forces of the universe go to work, and you need to do nothing else but allow. Focused intention and allow. That is the mantra / the new universal sound of manifestation, dear ones.

So take a deep breath and give yourselves a rest.

You have been doing much hard work, and now is the time to let us do the rest.

Allow us to bring you the dreams you have woven into the new stage of light.

Be still, be focused, and be in gratitude – stay in the light no matter what appears in the play called life. There is much falling away, much being re-purposed, re-focused and much gathering happening that you may never see.

Pay no mind to the outer dimensions for this reason. All is not as it seems. The illusion is falling away; let it fall - you do not need to engage in the drama of it all.

Keep your hearts safe and sound. Center yourselves and focus on the positive stuff. All that you want to draw in, not what you want to fall away or get rid of that, is already being taken care of.

Allow the hope to creep back into your thoughts - hope for the future, dear ones. The past is already gone; you are just witnessing the exit of all that is wrong / all that no longer fits must be witnessed not to draw you back in but to finally open your hands to release it.

Open your hands, stretch your arms out wide, and welcome in the future however you design / whatever you desire -

open your hands and allow it to be drawn deep inside; the manifestation starts within you, dear child.

For you are the holy of holies, the beacons of light, the harbingers, and creators of all you desire.

Welcome in the morning light. A new dawn is coming; in fact, it already is in the dimension of where you now reside.

Welcome in the coming tide – of blessings, of hope, of peace, and all that you decide.

Blessings, dearest children of mine, blessings to you from Mother Divine

What does this message mean to you?

What action or feelings does this inspire in you?

How can you bring the wisdom of this message into your daily life?

Witnessing the End of the Play

Holy Angels filled with light – love is the promise of breathing in new life – focus on the love in your hearts and let the rest fall away; the anger, the hatred, the violence, the struggle all is false evidence appearing real (fear), and there is no place for this anymore. This is the last hurrah. The last final remnants of all the sadness held within come to the surface to be cleared so that we can all begin again.

What you are witnessing is the ending of the play – the final climax before all is resolved and the love is able to shine once again like never before.

Bear witness to this and say 'never more, never more' – all that is ugly about this third-dimensional stage is being played out in its final days.

For there is evidence now that all is risen and moving up into the higher dimensions. If you have not yet cleared out your heart, you will feel the burden of these days most of all but remember, dearest children of light - that is what you are - you are the light, the way showers, the bright sparkles shining amidst the chaos that reigns and you are shining your light to allow the exit of these most disturbing rays (days).

Even if you feel at the moment, lower than low, depressed and in fear, overcome by anxiety and dread - these are the days that have been foretold - the revelation of what has been hidden coming up to be witnessed then released, and the room in your hearts will be filled with divine grace. It may be hard to see it right now, but all will be healed - by the thoughts and prayers of you all.

So hold onto your hats before the final show.

THE REBIRTH OF HEAVEN ON EARTH

Just as it all began with the 'Great Fall' – all shall now be healed by the rising of it all. The debris of doubt, fear, anger, discomfort, dis-ease, prejudice, and maladies of these dying days are rising up to meet the newly created heaven on earth and asking to be cleared for voices to be finally heard. And once the darkness rises up to meet the light, all will be healed in the blink of an eye.

Have faith, dearest warriors of the light; the blessings are flowing though all seems dark at this time.

Keep on praying, aligning with your light, and rising up in your own heart and mind.

Hold the masses in the palm of your hand and whisper words of light and healing to them. Send the light out into the world even if you don't feel you are up to it right now.

Keep going, keep the faith; that is the difference each one of you can make.

We are almost at the finish line, don't give up the race, keep on running, keep on jumping, keep on aligning with the Creator's light and vibration of the highest, and keep on keeping your eye on the prize - heaven on earth manifesting beyond the current time.

Clear your hearts of all that rises up, using the violet flame and the Angels of Heaven on Earth, and become the holy beacon that shines it's light no matter the outcome and without taking sides. Stay out of the fray and shine the light on all souls below, holding the energetic outcome that steals the show, appearing out of nowhere to guide you home.

THE REBIRTH OF HEAVEN ON EARTH

With love and great blessings, we stand by your side, in you, through you, and all around you, supporting you during these very difficult stages of becoming light.

> *We are the Angels of the Heavenly Realms, and we call upon you now to do what you came here to do – Be the light and shine bright dearest children of mine, shine bright with all the Angels of Heaven and I – for I AM Your Mother and You are ALL dearest children of mine*

What does this message mean to you?

What action or feelings does this inspire in you?

How can you bring the wisdom of this message into your daily life?

Merge into a New Understanding of Holiness

Holy child full of light – allow yourself to rest and be freed from the chains that bind you. A lot of healing work to be done tonight.

Allow your soul to rise into your sacred pyramid of light and be comforted by the human, angelic tribe and all of the legions of light while you sleep and dream tonight.

For in the dreamtime is where you create what will appear next in your life; it is also where you confront your fears and put them to bed by your bedside, dear child, for the boogeyman cannot exist if you do not believe in him, my dear. There are lots of misguided souls who tend to worry you and instigate fear, but nevertheless, you cannot let them 'get to you,' my dear.

THE REBIRTH OF HEAVEN ON EARTH

For in faith, there is a season for letting go, and this is the season, dear child – you cannot control the show, only the way you react to it – so come on, let's go on a journey full of de-light – the future you are seeking is ever so bright, shining light, shining light amid the debris of ancient sacrifice there is shining the brightest of lights – for God does not want you to shed blood in His name, and Mother the Holy Spirit wants to shine through you – this is the end game for the old ways. You must merge into a new understanding of the holiness that reigns within you and each and every soul who has been freed of this tiresome charade.

Like animals in a cage, you are waiting for the gatekeeper to come and release your chains. But child, you have already been freed; you just need to believe and be freed within the confines of the mind that creates the visions that you see in front of thee.

THE REBIRTH OF HEAVEN ON EARTH

Yes, this latest event has taken you by surprise. But have you ever wondered what you would see if given new eyes? Opportunity, dear child. For healing. For darkness to rise and be banished/absorbed/transformed into the light and freedom from darkness and all hidden crimes. That is the end goal. The end state we have in mind. Filling the world with its own bright light, shining through each and every one of you, one soul at a time.

These feelings of doubt and fear will not last, my dear. For when the weather turns rough, all will be cleared. Clearing the air of shadows and despair. Follow your heart, for we will lead you there - to the highest expression of love ever been released into the atmosphere.

Mother is here. Mother is here. Holding your hand and guiding you, dear.

Release and let go of all you do not know and allow the hands of faith to guide you safely home, into your heart streaming full of light - overflowing and sending out renewal, redemption, and freedom from fear, the dearest angel of mine.

For I AM your Mother - Your Mother Divine, and You are ALL precious children of mine

THE REBIRTH OF HEAVEN ON EARTH

What does this message mean to you?

What action or feelings does this inspire in you?

How can you bring the wisdom of this message into your daily life?

Finding the Oneness in You

Dearest children, holy and bright no matter the color or the tribe, you have all been made and embraced in my holy light. You are the magnificent and holy wonders of the universe, the holy angelic tribe of the human aspect of Mother / Father divine. You have come to Earth with a purpose, to heal and embrace the love in your hearts - reuniting all aspects of the divine within your hearts and minds. Oneness is the goal we ascend to - not that everyone is the same, but that unique differences could be embraced. Each is holy and beautiful in its own right. Each one is a facet of the whole, for streamers of light are each one of you as you dare to be bold. Each of you has a single strand of gold emanating a blessing for this world.

Dig deep in your hearts to find the oneness within. The ancient melodies of harmony enfolding and embracing you once again.

For it is enough to rise to the surface all that needs to be healed; wounds are now festering, waiting to be healed. Love and embracing is the only way to solve these ills. Not one of you is better than another; all serve a purpose, be not fooled. The ego wants to remind you of all that you do that is separate from the others. It divides you based on your differences; it is only God and the Holy Spirit that heal and bring you together to comfort and absolve you and make you once again healed and whole. Humanity as a species is beautiful. Surrounded by grace and full of love. So focus on the love, on the voices wanting to be heard, and allow this to guide you in a peaceful resolution of the shadow world.

For that is what you see before you – all that you are NOT. The opposite of who you truly are.

For deep in your heart, you know the truth; all that you want can be brought to you – healed in an instance of God's divine grace, lighting up the spark that defines you – your purpose, your passion aligned with God's will. That is the secret, the only one you need to know.

Align with the higher power, the highest expression of God's will – the one that helps and heals and has a solution for all. Then let go and allow the power and the blessing of God to work through you. Whether you believe in Heaven or Hell, in Church or Illusion, that is your will. Give up all notions of what you think is going on and sit in the stillness to find your way home, your next step, the piece of your soul you were meant to share with the world.

For all is an infinite puzzle waiting to behold. Each strand of gold, each mighty soul, is a reflection of God's highest love for the world. YOU are the blessing the world needs right now. YOU are the healing reflections of the new realm. Do not be afraid to shine your highest light - the world needs peace and blessings, and you have the means to make things right.

Align with Divine will, your highest possible aspect of self, and move the world into the higher realms with your intention, with your deeds, with the vision you hold for infinite beauty, and we will fill you / surround you in the Spirit of Grace.

For you are the masters, the keepers of the violet flame, the holy saviors riding in to save the day, but it will not be done from ego or from separateness, you see, it will be done from the higher aspects that are holy and free from apathy.

Love all kinds; all life is divine. You are brothers and sisters from one holy light – each of you holy and divine, each of you holy/whole in your own right.

Never forget the greatest rule of life – love each as yourselves, and it will be returned in kind. Treat others how you want to be treated, dear child. That is all and nothing more. It is really quite simple if you let it all go; that is the only rule you ever need to know.

With love and blessings on this joyful day – let us turn our hearts to the Spirit of Grace, to honor and respect the grace that is flowing now through the veins of time and allow the healing to begin from deep inside.

I am your Mother Divine, and I implore you to hear this message at this time

What does this message mean to you?

What action or feelings does this inspire in you?

How can you bring the wisdom of this message into your daily life?

Listen to the Holy Spark Deep Inside You

Holy children of the light – let the love shine through your hearts as you enter a new domain, one that is free and light and filled with love for every living creature in heaven on earth. As you were in the beginning, so shall you now return to be – bright and sunny and full of de-light, all aspects in harmony with the oneness of all life.

For in your hearts, you know it to be true; no matter the lessons you have learned, the scars you have bared, in your essence, the truth of who you still shine through. There is a holy spark deep within each of you.

Listen to your heart to feel the truth of this.

No matter who you are or where you have been now is your second or third chance to reveal your true essence. The inner majesty that glows brightly within, the God seed that burns like a magic flame, weaving ecstasy through your life whether you choose to envision it or not, there is a power that is flaming through you right now, a power you can harness to bring positive change about.

It is your job to witness the power, to direct it and manage it and play with it, to see the magic it can weave within you through you and all around you, dear children.

For you were born to play the music of the ethers dancing all day and singing praises to the heavens for the glory that it rains great big bouts of blessings – welcome in the change.

Let go of the drudgery, the skepticism, the delays and open the flame, the holy spark that burns within, to accepting this great change, a journey back to the golden days.

THE REBIRTH OF HEAVEN ON EARTH

For it is not in the future but in return to the beginning that you should now rejoice. The ending of a cycle, over 100,000 years in the making – the journey back to your holy essence that you now shall embrace, full of power, energy, streams of de-light, welcoming yourselves and calling it forth, the magic and the holy embrace of these the blessing times.

We are the Angels of Heaven, weaving in new light, breathing into the ethers the magical design of this, your brightest holiest light/life

What does this message mean to you?

What action or feelings does this inspire in you?

How can you bring the wisdom of this message into your daily life?

You Have Always Been Whole and Complete

Dearest child of light – the struggle for holiness, the wholeness that you crave, has from the beginning been the loneliest charade.

For you have always been whole, you have always been complete; there has been nothing missing. It has all been a charade, actively engaged in re-member-ing, collecting the pieces you thought had strayed when in fact, they have been inside you all the way.

Just breathe.

There is nothing for you to do. Just stay in the stream of grace that is currently surrounding you.

THE REBIRTH OF HEAVEN ON EARTH

Sit tight.

Open and breathe.

Release anything that has nothing to do with **Me** – your holiest center – the seat of grace.

Allow all else to leave. Allow it to leave and fill the space with grace.

Just breathe.

Breathe in the new, into the darkest space, and allow your light to shine forth, new light bright and shiny – just breathe. Two steps forward, now stop and breathe. Allow yourself to sit in the stillness and wait.

THE REBIRTH OF HEAVEN ON EARTH

Wait before you move forward again. All comes in stages, steps, not one big leap. A little at a time. That is what it takes. If you want to keep moving forward, take time to breathe and release all that you no longer need.

You are loved, you are cherished, and you are aligned – stay in alignment with the Divine, and all will fall into place.

Let go, breathe, and welcome me anytime.

With love and great blessings, I stand by your side,
Your Mother, Your Friend, dear Clementine

What does this message mean to you?

What action or feelings does this inspire in you?

How can you bring the wisdom of this message into your daily life?

The Gap is Closing Between Heaven and Earth

Dearest hearts – there is a distance now between you and the stars, and it is not so far off. The gap is closing, dearest children of mine. Each time your heart lights up, it raises the current vibration, and so you move into a higher dimension. Many of you have walked into a new dimension seemingly overnight.

Do you feel the lightness around you?

Have your hearts lifted up despite the appearances surrounding you right now?

This is cause for celebration, for transcending the lower vibrations and holding yourselves in a higher pattern, a higher instance of being, and a closer reality to be filled with love. This is the vision you are holding onto, and it is creating a new instance of reality to envelope you all.

For you are all Creators. Just because you find yourself in a current circumstance does not mean that it needs to continue in this manner. It does not mean that is all there is – there is so much more to discover, dear ones. Allow yourselves to explore, free from the burdens calling from distant shores. It cannot touch you anymore.

Allow your reality to explode in a version of de-light, joyful creations full of color and free from strife. There is no need to struggle against the waning, the lower vibration, for it is rising up, ready to become a higher / better version of itself, just like everyone else. The symptoms, the dis-ease, are what you see, but it is not reality. The reality is you are all rising up – the good, the bad, the ugly, and more – to be healed and cleansed and held in our loving arms.

THE REBIRTH OF HEAVEN ON EARTH

To start a new day with a fresh outlook and a higher level of light to guide you on your way. You are moving; you are rising; you are claiming a better way of life – a new way to embrace each other and to care for yourselves and to claim your birth rights – equal partners in this play called life. It is time to start a new chapter, turn a new page, and enter a dimension free from separation, free from fear and allowing all happy souls to dwell there. Your heart holds the key to the opening, and from there, you will be able to discern the truth behind all that is happening.

This is not the end; it is the beginning of something better, something new, something you will be able to hold onto. The past is just that, passed and gone; you are moving away from it, dear ones.

Do not wallow in sorrow or fear, for tomorrow is already here, and it is filled with the love of new dimensions, the abundance of all glory, and all that you have hoped and dreamed is opening for you to walk on through - to allow the blessings to shower over you.

All is not as it appears is the understatement of the day.

For we are showing you how to rise up into a higher state of mind. Releasing the shackles that have bound you here and rising into higher frequency patterns - releasing all fear and embracing the joy as you reside here, closer to your hearts and this thing you call love, opening the gates for your dear ones, opening the gates for your dear ones.

For now, it is the birthing of heaven on earth, and you are invited to celebrate with us, dear ones.

With love in our hearts, we surround you with light, holding the gates open for you to move forward and embrace your brightest life.

We are the Angels of Heaven, and we are surrounding you – opening your hearts and guiding your path forward at this time. Blessings, dearest children of mine, blessings of the holiest light – surrounding and protecting you, dearest holy beings of the highest light.

The Angels of Heaven and Mother Divine

What does this message mean to you?

What action or feelings does this inspire in you?

How can you bring the wisdom of this message into your daily life?

Change is in the Air

Dearest hearts – Change is in the air; can you feel it? It is coming, dear ones; the triumphant blare of the signal horn, the loud blasting lambasting of the less fortunate ones, is coming to an end, dear ones. Ushering in a time of healing for all involved, ushering in a time of reckoning, and recognizing all that has gone wrong. For this play is coming to an end, and another one is beginning, dear friends.

All that you have hoped and dreamed is coming to fruition; finally, it seems. And all that you have prayed for and thought was put on the shelf is coming to fruition right now. There has been much going on behind the scenes, many, many years in the making, and now you are seeing the change start to flow through, the veil of illusion, peeking through.

THE REBIRTH OF HEAVEN ON EARTH

It is time for the healing to begin. Time for the scars and the wounds to heal and for the people that surround you to come into unity - to be together as one, one nation under God - for everyone. Without struggle, without strife, without the major disasters that have been foretold of this time. We wish we could say it will happen overnight, easily with grace this time, but alas, it is up to each and every one of you to hold that in your hearts and minds.

A vision of loveliness we see for you - asking you to hold this vision too. Despite all the alarms that are ringing, the disasters the evening news is bringing, hold the Earth and all her people in your hearts and minds, one family, one tribe, one precious gift you are giving to mankind - this vision of embracing and cherishing each other as one - treating each other the way you would want to be treated dear ones, with LOVE. That is all there is and ever shall be; start to use your loving power wisely, and you will see the shift that is happening.

Embrace yourself, love yourself, be kind to yourself, and then start to bring the love out into the world. No more anger, no more fear; all that is left is to be kind, my dears (and dry your tears).

For enough is enough; the message has been heard, and hearts of love are healing all around the world.

Forgive and move on, for the future is bold, and you have already made it across the threshold of a new time, a new dimension, a new vision before you to hold onto. So hang your hats on the promises made and dare to start a brand new day - full of hope and blessings to you, full of the majesty that lies within you, in unity and grace and peace be bestowed; you are the blessing you wish to hold.

THE REBIRTH OF HEAVEN ON EARTH

Add your smile and your laughter, and you will avoid disaster, allowing your heart to heal and your mind to wander into new possibilities away from the crime, the negligence, and the lower-occupied signs of a vision of a world that is falling away, disintegrating you shall say.

Open your heart and your mind to a brand new way, and set the stage for the new play. All that has gone before you is washed away, and the remains of the day shall be to play, sing, dance, and more with laughter ringing across the shores of love and light and peace and grace. Allowing the angels to bring much praise.

Hold this in your heart, my dear friends, children no more are you – for you have graduated into a much higher standing, a level of new understanding, and now I embrace you and love you as one, a magical, mysterious element of love reaching out and touching your hearts, and I hear the love gushing forth as if from a wonder-us fountain of angelic grace, flowing over humanity and the human race.

Slow down and savor this heavenly dispensation of love, rearrange the flowers to absorb more light, and for mother nature to take a reprieve at this time.

With love in our hearts, from my soul to yours, you are the angelic kingdom here on Earth, and you are holding hands with me, my loves, your mother in spirit, dear holy ones. Sweet blessings to you, dearest children of light; for now, you are graduated into the new paradigm.

Farewell for now, but you know I never leave, for I AM a part of you as you are a part of me. Hold my hand as we walk through this thing called time, for the past is now disappearing, and you must let it go – reach for my hand, and you will know my presence before you, within you now, welcoming you into the new dimension, a place called LOVE, where EARTH becomes HEART and all is now well.

Blessings, dear ones; I love you all, for you are my future; I see you now on the other side of fear and embracing as one. I love you all, my dear ones.

> *For I AM your Mother Divine, and you are the angelic kingdom growing before my eyes*

What does this message mean to you?

What action or feelings does this inspire in you?

How can you bring the wisdom of this message into your daily life?

THE REBIRTH OF HEAVEN ON EARTH

Streamers of Love from Our Hearts to Yours

Dearest hearts – We come to you this day with love in our hearts. Sending you streamers of love from our hearts to yours. We can see you need some 'shoring up' – so many are discouraged and tired of waiting for change to take place; however, it all will change in but an instant while you are standing in the same place.

Never underestimate the power of global consciousness, dear ones.

For you have the power to influence it with your thoughts. The very fabric of reality is shifting beneath your feet. We cannot contain the power and rapidity with which this shift is happening. It is all very exciting – to see you standing in one realm and then shifting into the higher dimensions.

Right now is clean-up time, dear ones. There is much that has been left behind, and yet you must travel back and forth to assist in the clean-up of the lower realms. And that is why so many are so tired, dear ones. You are traveling and assisting in lifting others up, whether you know it or not.

For you cannot leave a mess behind, you must clear up as much as you can before you can be free of the lower dimensions.

For the 3D world continues to exist even though it may go on without you. There are many there reaching out their hands, ready to commence the climb into the $5^{th,}$ and they are looking for you to assist.

Just as your ancestors, masters, and guides reached out to help you, so shall you return the favor, dear children of mine.

THE REBIRTH OF HEAVEN ON EARTH

There are many that have been abandoned and abused, and they need help from you. Once you have realized a higher truth, once you are fully settled, you will be able to turn around and help the others who are found, who are reaching out and waiting to be seen / to be heard. There are the bells of freedom ringing now, dear ones. You will not want to leave them behind once you see the turning of the tide.

Stay vigilant in welcoming the blessed times. Do not fear the new truths you will hear but start to defend those you hold dear. Start to witness the problems you are trying to avoid. By witnessing and bringing these troubles into the public eye, we will start to heal the world, one soul at a time.

It is imperative that you understand what will come to pass will be difficult to see, but by witnessing it from the depths of your being, you will begin to understand the unraveling, and you will never again bear witness to such atrocities, for the healing will begin, and you will begin to understand the critical nature of God's divine plan to rescue from the entrenchment of the lower lands and to bring you into unity, into harmony with the higher dimensions. This is where you will be free to create from scratch the life you have dreamed of so many times and the ultimate culmination of many lifetimes.

Lessons have been learned, and you have been forewarned, rest now, dearest children of light, rest now, for you will need your strength as you move along the changing tide - of information, of witnessing great unrest and holding together the vision of true happiness. So that all who would have succumbed will be lifted in the grace of love and the barriers that blocked your climb will vanish in the blink of an eye.

For never again will you give your power away, never again will you be able to look away as troubles beckon you to do today. For you are the masters of the human race, and God has given you much grace.

You are surrounded by love and support from above. Continue the journey into the higher realms but look back and beneath you and embrace those reaching for help.

Spread your understanding, your knowledge, your good cheer, and allow the blanket of hope to bring you here, near to the heart of a loving God, embraced and whole dearest ones.

For we are here, cheering you on, we are here to help dear ones. Do not forget that we exist, and we exist in all holiness. For you are an extension of God's loving grace and your arms to be used to embrace.

Do not retreat in fear but allow our messages to carry you here – into the realms of heaven on earth, into the bountiful harvest you so deserve.

With love, light, and healing, the blessings begin – soon to embrace you and hold you, my dear friends.

This is your Mother Divine, and you are ALL special, precious children of mine

What does this message mean to you?

What action or feelings does this inspire in you?

How can you bring the wisdom of this message into your daily life?

Reach Forward, Rise Above

Holy children of the light, love is encompassing you all despite the many flagrant abuses of power that are rising to the surface for healing.

Dear child, it is up to you to hold the constant positive, loving vibe that will heal nations. Millions are counting on you, dear one. And we are holding you up. Encouraging you to 'rise above.'

Do not buy into the myths and drama and the dis-ease that is plaguing thee. Reach forward and keep your sights on the prize -earth where all life is cherished and embraced in the name of love and peace. There is a way to go before you get there, dear one but do not be fooled by outer appearances.

THE REBIRTH OF HEAVEN ON EARTH

The crimes against humanity that are surfacing now run very deep / very old / very oppressive. The energies will be heavily stacked against you, dear one, but you who hold the light of God close to you will be your source of power, your energy, and your faith. You must remain steadfast in the light regardless of what the rest of the planet looks like.

Mother Earth needs your compassion and your grace.

Allow the oxygen you breathe to be recycled for the highest and best of those who would love you into life, the mother that nurtures you, the father that holds you, and all of the many friends who surround you.

Be at peace, dear one, despite the swirl that moves around you. Stay centered. Stay in peace.

Allow the others to reel and be free in their expression of horror as the stories play out. It is important not to judge.

For you are a beacon of hope and love. All things can turn positive dear one. Look at all the lessons learned.

Embrace yourself, the darkness and all, for it is never too late to change, dear one. And that is what this is about, embracing the parts of self, of the world that surrounds us as reflected from your inner self to the change that needs to come about.

This has been a journey from darkness to light – you are so close, so close to walking forever in the light / the loving embrace of the Creator surrounds you now.

Keep on walking forward, dear one. Keep on walking on the bridge of light, connecting the dimensions, weaving the healing, purging the darkness, one soul at a time.

You are blessed and adored. It is time for you to freely explore all the healing that is in store.

> *With love and blessings, I AM Archangel Michael, Guardian of the Light, Protector of the Children of Mother/Father Divine, Beacon of Holy Light, and Embracing the Goodness of all Life*

What does this message mean to you?

What action or feelings does this inspire in you?

How can you bring the wisdom of this message into your daily life?

Time to Resurrect the Dreams You Left Behind

Dearest children – We are watching you in this time of change.

And what of it, dearest children of light? How are you seeing your life, and how do you spend your time? Are you changing anything, dear ones? Are you breaking free from the old routines and embracing what this time could mean? A chance to jump on all the hobbies you have put away, to exercise and clean and take a side trip down a country lane.

All of these things can be yours, my dear friends, the dreams you put on the shelf for another time when the time was rushed instead of felt.

It is time to resurrect the dreams you left behind and get back to you of your youth – the vibrant, energetic soul of a child. That is what I wish to impart to you today.

There is no more time to waste. Time is coming to an end, and all the dimensions to flow/blend together again, dear friends. So make the most of what you have and enjoy each and every moment of it.

It is time to play, to laugh, to dance, to sing – it is time for crafting and relishing the quietness inside.

No more rushing, no more worrying about what other people think – this time you are walking in is an extension of what was supposed to be – it was supposed to come all crashing down by now, and look what each new day brings, a chance to start anew, fresh perspective.

THE REBIRTH OF HEAVEN ON EARTH

So do not waste another minute, dear friends, do what you came here to do, and when Mother Earth sings you into the higher levels, do not forget the struggles you had here – for this is a school of healing, dear friends, a chance to leave all the lessons behind is beckoning to you, but first you must bide a little more time.

And when the new dimension comes fully into view, you will have new gifts that walk with you.

It is time now to put the rest to bed, the old, the ugly, the indifferent, and fully embrace the soul of love that beckons to you now – calling out to embrace the wonderful new start you have been waiting for, dear ones.

And in the meantime, enjoy the space and the comfort that surrounds you.

Rest in the knowing that the best is yet to come, and there is nothing for you to do to welcome it in than to relish the time you have here in this place, embracing all that you once were and all that you long to become.

With many blessings and surrounding you in the space of love, I AM Your Mother Divine, and you are all dearest children of mine

What does this message mean to you?

What action or feelings does this inspire in you?

How can you bring the wisdom of this message into your daily life?

You are the Light of a Thousand Suns

Holy child of love and light, you are the beacon of de-light. We hold you in our loving arms; our hearts are open wide, welcoming you, dear one.

For you are the light of a thousand suns.

Sit in the stillness of the moment and allow us to gather around you, dear one.

Feel our presence, our warm, loving embrace.

Feel the softness of our feathers upon your face.

Allow the warmth of our love to flow all around you, in you, and through you, dear one.

We are lending you our support.

Feel it.

Breathe in.

Rest in it, dear one.

We are lending you our loving light.

Rest.

Breathe.

Take comfort and refuge in love and the holy light that surrounds you, dear child.

Rest.

Breathe.

Allow the holiness of this moment to permeate each and every cell, every inch, every molecule, and every space in between – filled with the loving embrace, the holy light that shines from God above into your heart, your mind, and your body filled with light.

Allow God's love to flow into you now, dear child, wiping away any worry, fear, and dis-ease.

Comforting you in your time of need.

Peace.

Blessings flowing to you now, like the flowers that bloom and fall around you like rain bringing the fragrance of holy grace – light, free, filled with love – that is what we wish for you, dear one.

Rest.

Breathe.

Absorb this holy light, this holy moment that suspends all time.

Know your own worth – you are holy and divine, shining brighter than all the stars in a darkened sky.

Lighting up and uniting as one with your holy self, the center of love. Guiding, guarding, and embracing you, dear one.

> *For we are the Angels of Heaven, and You are the Holy Ones*

What does this message mean to you?

What action or feelings does this inspire in you?

How can you bring the wisdom of this message into your daily life?

The Veil has been Pierced and the Convergence Begun

Children of the holy light, we are lifting you up into our arms tonight. Heavenly Father and Mother Divine sending blessings to the human, angelic tribe.

For we have asked much of you as of late, so many of you have been lending your energy to the changing tide – through your prayers, your dreams, and your holy light. And heaven thanks you for welcoming her in to see the state you have been living in.

The veil has been pierced, and the convergence has begun.

For heaven and earth are bound to be one.

THE REBIRTH OF HEAVEN ON EARTH

And as this heavenly shift occurs, know that you have played an important role in the shifting of heaven on earth.

And as the world continues to embrace the holiness and the rage, you are witnessing the end of final days – as it was in the beginning, so shall it now be – full of grace with angels taking their rightful place as the leaders of love and light, so many of you are examples learning to shine their own light, and we welcome you now dearest children of light into the embrace of the loving inside your hearts and minds.

For what flows within will shine now.

It is time for all your walls to come down.

It is time for you to stand up in the name of love and embrace the destruction of all that stands in the way of that now.

THE REBIRTH OF HEAVEN ON EARTH

All conflict, all wars, all rage - time for it to be put away, to be absorbed into the realm of love, and to be certain that all who are wounded care for dear ones.

For you know the way. You have been practicing for many, many decades.

It is not what it looks like, dear ones.

The rage is rising up to be heard, but it is not growing; it is on its way out, and the underlying problems are about to be solved. With the arrival of the heavenly ones, you will no longer be denied the applause. The world will stand in wonder and awe, and all will be washed away / cleansed in the holy rays; as love shines down stronger than before, you will witness the change in miraculous ways.

THE REBIRTH OF HEAVEN ON EARTH

We love you, We bless you in infinite ways, for we are the Angels of Heaven welcoming in brand new days. With love and blessings from our hearts to yours, you are the Angels we are calling forth.

What does this message mean to you?

What action or feelings does this inspire in you?

How can you bring the wisdom of this message into your daily life?

The Universe is an Infinite Canvas on which to Create

Legions of light are surrounding you, dear child and every child on earth at this moment is on the cusp of the major transition from darkness into light.

For many are walking among you, albeit out of sight. This is the Galactic Federation of Light, and we are welcoming you into the fold tonight. There is much to share and so much wisdom we can impart but for now, just know that our light and our arms are enfolding you, dear child.

The universe is a wide open space, an infinite canvas on which to create, and the beginning is just now happening – a fresh start, a brand new world opening up.

It is yours to create.

THE REBIRTH OF HEAVEN ON EARTH

We are waiting for you to step forward with your paint, your brush, and your infinite light – lending your voice to the human, angelic tribe.

We are watching for the light to appear; we can see you walking en masse and yet still a distance away.

We are calling out to you, sending you signs of what is ahead, but alas, you are not there yet.

But you are closed, and the door is open now, and some of you will be arriving very shortly. We can see your individuated forms breaking free from the group, and your light is shining and moving forward. There are so many secrets to share. So many legions are watching you, waiting to make contact with you.

Despite what you have been told, it is not us that will appear in your world. It is you that are walking across the divide into ours – out of the matrix of time and into the universal fold of the new that you will create. You are taking down the dividers / the walls of illusion built around you, and then suddenly, you will see what / who has already and always been around you.

For we have always been in your world, but you shut us off / cut off contact, but now you are rising up. And so 'first contact' will not come from us; it has already been coming from us, and as soon as you can see, it will be coming from you. You are walking toward us, out of the matrix of separation and into the realms of love.

We welcome you, dear ones. We are waiting.

Keep on walking toward us. There are so many of us that want to connect with you, to be acknowledged by you, for we have been waiting for you. Not you for us but us for you. We cannot wait for you to arrive, to cross the heavenly divide, and to welcome our world into your hearts and minds.

Blessings, dear child – we are waiting for you.

The Galactic Federation of Light

What does this message mean to you?

What action or feelings does this inspire in you?

How can you bring the wisdom of this message into your daily life?

THE REBIRTH OF HEAVEN ON EARTH

You are Leaps and Bounds from Where You Started Out

Angels from heaven are showering you with blessings, dearest children of the light.

For in your hearts, we see so much peace, albeit what is showing up before you is much dis-ease.

This dis-ease comes from the misalignment of the outer and inner worlds. What once was commonplace no longer resonates with you. You are starting to question everything and everyone around you.

When you get that uncomfortable feeling in the pit of your stomach, stop for a moment.

Check in and breath.

Call on us for help to bring you more at ease. And ask to be shown what the misalignment is about that you are feeling. Ask for help in rearranging events to be more in line with who you are now.

For each of you has grown in more ways than one, more growth than in any other lifetime just in the last few months, dear ones. You are leaps and bounds from where you started out.

The world is not the same as it was a few months ago, dear ones. And so the disconnect may widen for some of you, and that is okay; know that who you are and where you want to be will begin to narrow the divide - it may be somewhat slow and subtle this change you are in right now, or it may come in roaring like a lion. However, the change appears; know that you are protected.

THE REBIRTH OF HEAVEN ON EARTH

Many of you are aware of the changes that are coming but not yet consciously - to bring your awareness into the tight spaces, the lonely places, will bring much reward - a fully conscious human being moving forward, clearly, directly, without holding back.

For the way forward is one of unity and grace, the reconciliation of lifetime plays. Healing the space in between and forging forward completely - your whole self, beaming with new sensibilities, new talents, new speed.

For you are heading for the speed of light - you are taking off like a rocket ship set on fire - holy and wise and ready for the next step, even if you do not consciously know it yet.

And we are here to guide you the rest of the way.

Use us. Reach out to us. Listen for our voice. Watch for the signs to guide you on the highest plane. For we are ready to assist.

We already see you in the healing mists, walking toward us, holding hands, resting, and healing as you walk the pathway into the higher dimensions.

And we wait to be of service.

Penelope, Angel of Grace

THE REBIRTH OF HEAVEN ON EARTH

What does this message mean to you?

What action or feelings does this inspire in you?

How can you bring the wisdom of this message into your daily life?

We are Holding You

Dearest heart – we know you for who you truly are. All of the entrapments of the earthly sojourn are gone, and you are free to roam – to satisfy the longing / the belonging – it's all gone, the struggles washed away, and the angst disappears at the end of the day.

For you have journeyed so far with us. Held our hands even as your tears were not yet dried, and in the end, you have mastered/conquered the divide.

In the end, we will all hold hands, and a symphony / a choir of angels will sing in the distance. And we will be holding you still as we always do, and fading remnants of the days long past will come back to you in all their vibrancy, and still, we will be holding you.

THE REBIRTH OF HEAVEN ON EARTH

For dearest heart, a dearest heavenly creature of light, your inner majesty is growing out of spite, for as the world appears darker and darker, you are becoming lighter and lighter. The darkness lifts off, and in its place, all you will find is love and light.

Blessings, dear child – be at peace and know we are here for you every step of the way.

Keep on keeping on, as they say, staying centered, and all the world will move around you, and you will stand in place, but when you fully wake up, you will realize the world has become an entirely different place.

For you are an angel as sure as these outstretched wings of mine, and now you have become a glorious and holy beacon of God's light.

Blessings, dearest child. Blessings of light. Sharing in the holy symphony tonight.

For you are a messenger of the human, angelic tribe, and we have enjoyed sharing with you in the holiness tonight.

> *I am Josie of the Angelic Realm, and I wish you could see the glory we see surrounding you now.*

What does this message mean to you?

What action or feelings does this inspire in you?

How can you bring the wisdom of this message into your daily life?

Waiting for Your Hearts to Re-Align

Dearest of hearts, the light shining from you mirrors the stars. We are watching you and waiting once again for the hearts to align to deepen our connection with humankind. We are standing in the midst of the grand turning point, dear children.

Like a massive ship, it does not turn all at once but takes a few tries before it rights its course. You are right now in the middle of the storm. The eye of the needle gets squeezed from both sides. And now, we are waiting for your hearts to re-align. The glory of heaven – watching and waiting, dear friends.

And what will you decide? To continue to rise higher in vibration, closer to the heavens? Or to divide and separate and scatter among the masses? What is your choice at this time? Unity or division? Wholeness or separation?

The outcomes are being built. Time for you to align. Bringing everyone together or letting things slide back into the abyss of the infinite mind.

The sounds you are making - wonderful sighs as you see the future you have created in your glorious eyes. You are almost there. Keep on walking forward. Missteps are no longer allowed - you will be picked up and carried by the crowd. So rejoice in your knowing that the blessing times are coming - in fact, you can see them starting to emerge from the debris of hatred in your world.

For what goes down must come back up - fruitful laboring and tending to brush, the forest glows with so much traffic, a fruitful bounty, the heaven-sent smorgasbord of positive intent. And the growth spurts forth to cover the mirth. The laughter of a merciless Lord lingers no more.

For in this space between worlds at this time, there are heavenly creations of power quite alive. Holy, divine, joyful creations bridging time, conquering the divisions of your current life. The lines of separation are about to disappear, with all the world holding its breath to see what comes next. It is time for you to see the light. It is time for you to climb the mountains that divide. It is time to put your swords down and embrace the fruitful mind.

How can you help make a difference my child?

By standing down from any events/arguments. By refusing to enter the exit – don't go back in through doors that have closed. Keep on walking forward.

See how you can recommend a change in direction toward unification, not separation. Stay centered in your own desperation, apart from the commiserating nations, and hold the flame of hope for a better tomorrow.

For the curtain is closing – the janitors are clearing the clutter so the stage can be reset. A new story to unfold, blessings to behold. Do not be afraid to be bold.

With love and blessings, we are here by your side – the Angels of the Heavenly Realms and the Hosts of Hope

THE REBIRTH OF HEAVEN ON EARTH

What does this message mean to you?

What action or feelings does this inspire in you?

How can you bring the wisdom of this message into your daily life?

The Creation Spins Again and Again

Beacons of hope, lights upon the darkest ropes - streamers lit up like the stars in the heavens, great strands of light reaching out from your world to mine.

For we are all connected, connections are coming up online (lights turning on, circuits being restored). Soon the communication lines will stream forth, fully restored, and the glory of the universe will expand forward, with Earth in her rightful place streaming alongside the other holy beacons lighting up the night sky.

And the citizens of Earth, you shall rejoice in knowing the faultiness of the darkness from which you have come. The sight of the heavens to shine forth and welcome you into the holy birth.

For Creation spins again and again, always moving forward and awakening. There is so much to learn and so much to see. You are giving birth to infinity / infinite possibilities.

Never fear the darkness as it descends, for there is no beginning and no end, just friends to share with and laugh with and cry your way through to the other side that is waiting for you. It is not dark here; there is no despair. The rules have all been changed, and the world has become fair.

For in the holiest host of truth, there is only one YOU, and YOU are all you are to be; in each and every moment, you are free, you are holy, and you are part of me.

Alcyone of the Central Sun

What does this message mean to you?

What action or feelings does this inspire in you?

How can you bring the wisdom of this message into your daily life?

Grand New Opening

The universal creation station up here in the heavens is ablaze in all its glory with the many possibilities of this grand new opening. Hearts to God and hands to work, reveling in the magic of this new universe.

For you have awakened an opening where doors have been shut for millennia of angels, have been guarding and guiding you back to this place, the rebirth and regrouping of the family of love within the space of heaven returning to earth.

For as the gates were shut to heaven and hell, leaving you in purgatory all its own, now the return is being blessed and healed, and the gates to heaven are opening once more. St. Peter and his legions of light are welcoming back the human, angelic tribe. Shut out from the Garden of Eden no more; your journey is safe and has been implored by many an angel and spirit guide – to allow humanity back inside. And now you are here; the gates have been unlocked. Slowly they start to open and let you back inside, into the sacred heart of the Creator's divine light.

Blessed be who comes to be among friends; all of the divisions have come to an end. The illusion had died; time to say goodbye and welcome in a brand new, free-falling, fully supported, and infinite light.

Journey safely, away from drama, suspended in a state of Grace, the angels of heaven one on each side, gathering around now to guard and to guide. Safe passage to the 'other side' of love and light – with ease and grace and trauma-free.

Blessed Be, Blessed Be, Blessed Be..
Archangel Metatron to Comfort Thee

What does this message mean to you?

What action or feelings does this inspire in you?

How can you bring the wisdom of this message into your daily life?

The Time has Come to Unveil the Secret Ones

Dearest hearts, the time has come to unveil the secret ones – the ones walking amongst you and yet hidden in plain sight – the angels, the masters, and the guides.

For so many have been following you, and now it is time for them to step into the forefront and lead, to turn on the lights hidden deep inside. Some of them are you, and some of them merely walk around you, hidden and unseen.

When the lights turn on, all will change.

You will be awakened within a day.

THE REBIRTH OF HEAVEN ON EARTH

One day, one night, and all the world will be filled with delight. Sorrows of the past washed away in the stream of everlasting light and the blessings that we bring.

For one by one, you will be saved, surrounded by the blessings of the heavenly rays.

For all that the Creator has sent forth is coming to you now, reaching and dismantling all discord. Releasing you from karmic bonds. Lifting you into a higher state of Creator light. Allowing healing from deep inside. Surrounding you now and sending you love and light, we are the Creator's light, and we are sending streamers of heaven to you tonight.

Rest. Absorb. Hold all in high accord.

Allow yourself to experience the love and blessings – the angels holding you in a sweet embrace, healing the wounds,

THE REBIRTH OF HEAVEN ON EARTH

and suspending all in a state of grace. For you have been saved, and you are safe.

Bask in the love of the Creator's light and know that now, finally, we are on your side.

There is nowhere to go but up this time, allow and release and be at peace.

With love and blessings from Mother Divine, you are human angels shining bright – holy and wise in your own right.

What does this message mean to you?

What action or feelings does this inspire in you?

How can you bring the wisdom of this message into your daily life?

Heaven is Waiting for You with Open Arms

Dearest hearts - Heaven is waiting for you with open arms, alive and well, and walking through the heavenly realms are millions of angels ready to welcome you home.

No, this does not mean you are going to die - it means you are being welcomed into everlasting life. You are transcending/ascending into the heavenly realms as you stand on your Earth, Mother, and are completely unaware of all that is going on behind the scenes. Like the puppet masters of the grand stage, there are others who are pulling all the strings that you cannot see. One knows not of the grand scheme and how it all will end But what you do know is how to feel and live and breathe, and you know that it has been very difficult for many lately.

And you know that you are clearing all that has gone before you, all that has 'passed away,' and now you are walking onto center stage. No one knows the lines of the script that will be placed before you; all you know is what has come before / what has left or is leaving, nothing more.

And soon you shall find with de-light, the flames of the elixir of life breathing new blessings into your life, replacing all that has gone before with the light of the heavens to explore – walking into a new dimension with your hearts and hands lifted to heaven. When friends and family and angels surround, you out in the open, hands outstretched, it will feel as though you never left.

A few more hurdles to cross. A few more crosses to bear – the fear that is leaving will cause an uproar, and that is when we need you to stand still. To stand in the faith of the ages that you have built, to rest in the reassurance that all is quite well. To stand for the resolution of all the past ills, to light the way for others to comfort themselves. For you are the way showers, the forbearers of the changing tide, and you the hope, the blessing where you reside. It is up to you to stand in your power and conquer all that divides, opening hearts and minds to the great turning, the great changing, the immense and enormous undertaking for the path has been set, and you are walking through it as we speak.

And when all changes, as if in the blink of an eye, you will be welcomed, you will be standing by our sides, just as we see you, you shall see us too, and then when the mist of illusion clears, you will see us standing here, right next to you, holding you close, with the legions of heaven with great toast – heralding the inner magnificence that made this change possible, heralding the gates that have been opened and ushering you into the halls of justice. Through the gates where Peter wept, into the path of least resistance, you are swept, and all that has been and ever will be known to Thee.

For you are a Creator light, and you are creating the turning tide. You have declared and decreed liberty, and for that, you are sent the Angels of Infinity. Looping around you as they may, weaving a batch of extraordinary light, for you are to live a wonderful life. For this is the rebirth of heaven on earth, and you are most decidedly close right now, hold on, for the ride may be rocky, but the vision stays still. Keep your eye on the prize and your heart full of hope as we, the Angels of Heaven, welcome you now.

With love and blessings, we bid you adieu – The Angels of Heaven welcoming you home to the life you were meant to live all along

What does this message mean to you?

What action or feelings does this inspire in you?

How can you bring the wisdom of this message into your daily life?

The Light is Working Overtime Right Now

Child of light, you are not the only one crying in this dark night, for much would appear that the light has disappeared, and yet that is not fathomable, my dear. The light is working overtime right now, blessing the darkness and healing the cabal.

For all that is fallen is not always lost; there are routes of redemption no matter the cost. The light is shining brighter than ever before, healing old wounds and releasing the dark from its horrible past.

For the ones that are shining are those that have been healed. Those that seek comfort in the release of the darkness harbored within are filling the empty spaces with love and light.

THE REBIRTH OF HEAVEN ON EARTH

Forgiveness is the theme that comes to mind.

For casting out the darkness from your life is all right, but then you have to heal the darkness and fill the empty spaces it was carried in.

Allow the light of the angels to come to you now, great wands of crystalline light entering the dark spaces and filling them with light. That is how we heal you and bring you back into the light by releasing all that is not right and filling the empty spaces with angelic healing swords of light. Majesty and grace beckon you now. Now that you have healed from tremendous sorrow.

Allow us to show you that all is not lost; this is merely moving through the dark spots. The spaces in your heart and mind that have been holding lessons in karma since the beginning of the end of time. We are nearing the space where all timelines collide; in oneness, we all will reside. It is time to clear the path and fill it with light. And it all starts with the journey deep inside.

When you go to your temples of light in the evening or before bedtime, ask the legions of heavenly hosts, the angels, the guides, those you love most - to join you there for a journey through space and time, a revelatory look at all your lives and gather the pieces of your souls that need to heal and bring them into the sanctuary with you. Hold them up to the light and ask the legions of angels to reveal the spark of the divine within each and every one of them - and when the wand touches you, all will be healed, all will be brought back to their original form, and light will shine from within each and every one.

For the light of the wand belongs to God, and the light from within is the connection it wants. So watch them light up, each and every piece of the whole, making its way from darkness back to home. The home is within your very soul, the fragments of light rejoicing in you as these pieces of darkness make their return to you. They are returned in the mist of golden white light and are glowing within, lighting you up from the inside out. A magical forest of fireflies dancing around, joining you deep down. Into the depths of your soul and the bottom of despair do they travel, making a path of light from which there was none, revealing the beauty of the soul from which they have come until all is one. One magnificent shining light, blended in the beauty, the holiness (wholeness) of unity, of majesty, of God's loving grace.

All is forgiven.

For the human race is one of a kind. The emotions, the intellect, and the divine mind. Warriors of the light, you have fought for millennia, and we have heard your cries. It is time now to conquer the divide. And we do this by healing you from the inside. For the light shines through the blessings old, every nook, every cranny, every fold – the oneness of your being can never be old, for it shines now with the light of a healed and everlasting soul, and the darkness that once unfolded has changed once again into the light of old (the original light of your soul), and it shines brighter than even the stars can begin to comprehend.

The light of the majesty once hidden shall rise again. Spreading its love, spreading its light over the evening in a bed of de-light. For in the morning, when you shall awake, you will recognize your daytime as your dream state. And all will be changed, rearranged.

So dry those tears that you cry. We have a plan in place, Your Mother, Your Father, Your Spirit Guides. The Masters of Creation ever so wise. We are your ancestors, your creators, your shining light, and we are sending you tremendous healing – remember to go there, in what you call your dreams, and we will tend to you in healing, sending many blessings. In peace, love, and light, we are your scribes – the holy, the nimble, and, yes, the wise.

Trust in me as I trust in you, and together we will pull you through the tunnel of darkness into a brighter life. In comfort and peace, we bring this healing to you, a gift from Mother Nature. God bless you.

The Angels, the Fairies, the Fireflies

What does this message mean to you?

What action or feelings does this inspire in you?

How can you bring the wisdom of this message into your daily life?

Timelines Converging

Dearest children of the heavenly light, we are fostering hope of joy, peace, and happiness within you at this time.

For the energies that surround you are of many conflicting waves of light, up and down, and all around, there is a mismatch of vibration – that is the reason for all the discord, too many timelines converging all at once. Those of the lower vibrations reaching up and pulling you down, others coming in sideways and pulling you off center. Brush yourself off, stand up proud and tall, and set your intention to align with the holiest (highest) of the vibrational currents swimming before you right now.

Jump up onto the highest wave and ride it into a state of ecstasy and grace. Allow the current to carry you home, rolling with the waves great and small, and take the lesson every surfer knows, you ride the wave, and you stand strong in the face of the currents that can take you under. You get up on the surfboard every time you fall, and you continue to ride the waves, each and everyone until you are carried home. Rough waters make people tougher, but you never see the surfer waiver; they keep swimming and keep riding one wave after another, enjoying the challenge, the grace, and the beauty of the water. And that is how we see this time you are passing through now – a tunnel of waves and water, of energy that flows up and down and all around, and we are asking you now to embrace the ride, get out your surfboard, and dive into the unchartered waters and have faith in the wind, the sun, the moon, the energy underfoot and overhead to guide you / to carry you home – to the peace in your heart and the stillness deep within that knows everything is not as it appears but that it will be okay once the atmosphere clears.

THE REBIRTH OF HEAVEN ON EARTH

For there are great waves of light washing over you now, in you, through you, and all around. Breathe with it, do not hold it in; the air needs to release so you can keep breathing in. Do not be afraid. Do not cower in fear. The heavenly realms are supporting you, dears.

Allow all hurt and sorrow to pour forth, great cleansing and purging of all that has come forward.

Many tales are to be told about these days of old in the generations that come – of how their ancestors breathed new life into Mother Earth and the call was heard to keep moving forward. Great strength and determination in the face of travesty rising to the surface.

So let it out, let it go, and allow a million streams of light to flow and illuminate the path of the everlasting soul.

For you are not your bodies, you know. You are pure light - so let go and let it flow to heal the ones in need of grace.

Light shining from your temples, your eyes, your crowns of gold. Light shining from your hearts, blessing the entire world.

Let the love and light of Mother / Father God shine through you, for that is what you are - a beacon, a lighthouse, a shining star - blazing forth with the Glory of the Heavens to release what no longer matters.

Let it go and move ahead; soon, you will see dry land, and you will step onto a space sacred and divine where all there is a light that shines, you will feel the burdens lift off your chest, and you will lay down your swords and rest. For peace is all there is.

THE REBIRTH OF HEAVEN ON EARTH

In majesty, grace, and the journey within – we bring you healing and an end to suffering, dear friends. Open your hearts, embrace our light, and together we will shine, shine, shine.

We are the Angels of Heaven, strong and wise, and we are standing by your sides.

What does this message mean to you?

What action or feelings does this inspire in you?

How can you bring the wisdom of this message into your daily life?

THE REBIRTH OF HEAVEN ON EARTH

Entering the Center of Universal Rebirth

Dearest Angels of Heaven and Earth - we are entering the center of the universal rebirth, and the labor pains are showing themselves in many ways - from the fires that rage on center stage - emotional, political, and earthly fires rage with flames shooting up and flowing forth in terms of words, actions, and emotional imbalance. This is the calming before the real storm flows forth. The blazes in the pacific northwest are what you call symbolic of the many fires raging within human consciousness.

And what you will see in the coming days are the outlets / the outpouring / the letting of the letting go when all that flows before you is the stuff that you need to let go of - many scenes of anger, deceit, hurtful beliefs will flow all around you, and it will seem there is no good to turn to, you may want to ditch and run, but there is no higher ground upon which to stand and then you will stand there in the midst of all of it, the chaos swirling around you, and you will find your soul.

You will finally hear the inner urgings taking hold.

You will be able to listen in the calm amidst the storm and find you that you have been looking for all along.

The curtains will open, the veil will depart, and the wisdom you have been searching for will be all you can see – all you want to do will be to embrace the others around you; the ego is gone, the searching, the feeling so lost – all of it will disappear, and you will be left standing there. On top of the mount, the highest of solid ground, you will be witnessing the greatest human event ever could be found.

The return to love.

THE REBIRTH OF HEAVEN ON EARTH

The journey has been long and hard, and we have journeyed with you, dear ones. We have seen hearts torn apart. We have witnessed the grinding of the energies as of late. We have whispered in your ears, sometimes too late.

And now is the time for the sweet embrace.

It is time to let go.

The final letting before the storm shall pass.

Opening the doors to the heavens at last.

For we are standing here with you, holding down the fort, and we are waiting for you to witness a great turning of the tide, for all you have known, all you have believed is all about to turn inside out, for what lies in deceit will come out and all that you have known all along is what has been inside, burning an ever-changing light and all will come out from the inside to make it all right.

Turning it right side up and inside out until the light that is shining dimly within is shining ever brightly without - guarding your path, guiding you along, it will be easy to see this light shining forth, and you will know without a shadow of a doubt that you are the beacons we are writing you about.

For you have had the light all along, You have had the opportunity to confront the shadows following you along, and you have been graced with the power of love to carry you dear ones. Do not forget the secret is love; that is all you have ever known in the true reality that is to carry you home.

Blessings of love to you, dearest souls of light; the change is coming, and we are standing by your sides. In the midst of the storms, you will find your light, and you will beckon to us, and we will strengthen your light, and you will be forevermore standing in God's holy embrace, birthing the new beginning from your inner strength.

With love, light, and blessings, peace be to you, the holy, the wise, and the true – for we are the Guardians of the Light, and we are sending you healing and grace, and peace tonight.

What does this message mean to you?

What action or feelings does this inspire in you?

How can you bring the wisdom of this message into your daily life?

The End of One Age and the Entering of the Next

Dearest children, we are approaching the end of the line, so to speak, the ending of one age and the entering of the next. Time will move more swiftly as old timelines intersect and collapse. Many of you have felt the swaying of the timelines and the coordinated integration of many timelines into several more promising prospects. This is by design, dear ones. The collapsing of the most fearsome into the higher level realms. Condensing the prospects so that it is easier for you to choose. Laying the foundation of a brand-new world.

The girders are in place to hold up the charade, but they will be tumbling down, the center faced. The election in the United States has taken center stage, but the focus is on the ongoing charade. What you see is not necessarily what you get. You must read between the lines to become versed in what comes next, for it is not pretty on either side. There is no savior coming to save the day. It is up to you to focus on the higher realms, the highest possible outcomes, and to send that energy moving forward.

You cannot look at what has happened in the past. You must make a reckoning with the choices before you, and you can only base it on what you know. We wish the information coming forward would burst forth, but as it is happening in 'real-time,' God only knows its worth.

The magic and the mystery of the heavens will light the way, but the hand on the ballot may not make mistakes. You will be overlighted with the choice that is right for you, based on the timelines surrounding you. There are many choices and many outcomes, but one thing is for certain, the world will never return to such a place, never return to this - center stage.

So go deep within and lay the choices out before you. Let your heart decide what is right for you.

Lay down your swords and your weapons of words and allow the stillness deep inside to guide you along.

Trust in the highest possible outcome for all involved, and you will not be allowed to go wrong.

The world before you deserves all voices to be heard. Those you agree with and those to learn from. There is not one right or wrong, but many possible outcomes, dear ones.

Allow your inner voices to be heard – the parts of you who have learned over eons of time to go within and conquer the mind. So vote with your hearts and allow the rest to rest.

For it is time to usher in peace, love, and happiness.

Take a break and wait for your next step.

We are the Angels of the Higher Realms, connecting with you during the night as you sit in slumber and rest; we are guiding your hands to do the rest.

What does this message mean to you?

What action or feelings does this inspire in you?

How can you bring the wisdom of this message into your daily life?

The Heavens have Opened a Spirit of Grace

Dear ones, so much have come to pass since we spoke last. Allow the opening in your heart center, in your universal truth center, to guide you as to what comes next.

For the heavens have opened a spirit of grace to flow alongside you as you encounter all that is now laid before you.

Streams of information flowing. Long buried secrets re-surfacing.

Take a deep breath, stay centered, and focused on your own happiness. Let us do the rest.

THE REBIRTH OF HEAVEN ON EARTH

For it has taken many eons to get to this place. Back to zero point. The grand awakening is taking place to reroute and re-direct the human race.

For it has been a race against time, a race back to the origins from which you came, back to the beginning to reset the stage. And this is the final scene / the final stage of this final play.

Hands are tied. Watch what comes next.

Get out your popcorn, and set your DVD player to record, for never before have you seen a showdown like this. Evil is routed out, and a new stage is now set. Both sides are enthralled in the scenes that are set forth – humanity coming together – one huge loving and healing force.

For the farce is over. No more pretending.

Let go of your swords, your words, all that divides.

For now, is time for coming together on both sides.

The duality has emerged as God's final word embraces the masses who deserve the truth and the joyful resonance of unity coming across the faces, the hearts, and the minds of all who are now separated by the grand divide – no matter the race, the creed, the color and all other divisions that now reside in your hearts and minds.

For God is light, the power of the breath, the seed of joyful happiness.

All is restored now as you wake up and find the darkness that has held power over your life is gone now forever, receded into the recesses of a distant memory, and all that appears now is the dream of ecstasy – of peace, of grace, of harmony.

The resonance filled in your memory / the memory of your cells and the light that lives between – the nature of this resonance is exhilarating / deafening the doubts that rage across your ego mind, creating the harmony through the energy that surrounds you, through your very soul, uniting within you the mind and ego / the spirit and the selfless parts of you working in harmony with all the rest of you.

For united we stand, divided we fall – that is the harmonic motto for all, not just in the United States but across the world. The masses will stand together as one, and that is how you change your world.

THE REBIRTH OF HEAVEN ON EARTH

We grant you many blessings, dearest warriors of the light, children from heaven standing in de-light. Hand in hand and heart to heart, opening up to the blessings pouring forth.

We see it, we feel it, we dream it into being for you, and the children of heaven are watching you.

Welcome, dearest children of love, into the rebirth of heaven on earth. Peace be with you and kindness your guide, opening all your hearts and minds, crossing the divide and bridges being built. We love you, We watch over you, We stand beside you in harmony and grace – sending blessings of love and goodness to the human race.

THE REBIRTH OF HEAVEN ON EARTH

Blessings of love from our hearts to yours – the Angels of Heaven here for you now, integrating our harmonic vibration into the fabric of your world so that all will awaken to the peace of love, the joy of grace, and the essence of human kindness taking over the stage.

What does this message mean to you?

What action or feelings does this inspire in you?

How can you bring the wisdom of this message into your daily life?

Breath in the Newness, Set Your Intention

Dearest child of light –the world is changing in every morning light. Each time the sun shines upon you, it makes the world brand new.

Breathe and allow the newness to settle over you.

Breathe and set your intention, and allow the universe to know what you want it to do. Give the energy direction. Each moment is malleable, changeable, with your every thought.

Set your intentions every morning.

Create what you want.

You are not a victim of any circumstance.

THE REBIRTH OF HEAVEN ON EARTH

You have the power to create worlds.

Give it a chance.

The universe is listening. Tell it what you wish it to grant.

The energy needs direction so it knows where to flow. Allow it to flow in the direction of your own creation, not anywhere else.

All of it is amorphic.

Floating through the air.

Allow it to share with you the desires placed there; focus your intention on this cloud of de-light, positive, radiant, iridescent with the potential / the desire / the new world made manifest.

THE REBIRTH OF HEAVEN ON EARTH

Set your intention in this beautiful, glorious iridescent bubble of Creator light and allow it to float in front of you for a while.

And as you envision this glorious, radiant bubble full of all that you desire, the possibilities emerge fully formed and float toward you to be absorbed into your own radiant field of light, a message from heaven filtered into your crystalline web of light, your own inner matrix of de-light. Allow this to happen.

Allow yourself to absorb the magical light of your own Creation.

And know that with each vision you set, each molecule of energy that you absorb, the miracle has formed.

Accept nothing less.

Allow your soul to rejoice in happiness.

Just rest.

Allow the magic to occur – the energy sent forth to manifest, floating on bubbles of joy and happiness.

Absorb and rest.

Accept nothing less.

This is the magic of creation, bubbles of laughter floating in on the breeze; the sun is shining, extending its creative energy.

Rest. Absorb. Allow.

Blessings, dear ones – life is easy at last; life is built on these bubbles of happiness.

> *I Am Your Mother Divine sending you / extending you / introducing you to your own inner magic, the ability to create miracles in your own lives.*

What does this message mean to you?

What action or feelings does this inspire in you?

How can you bring the wisdom of this message into your daily life?

Keep the Lamp of Faith Well Lit

Dearest children of the heavenly light – There is much going on in the inner world as you sleep at night. You are traveling inter-dimensionally, sharing insights so lovingly. For as you learn your lessons on this planet of love, you translate them into many other worlds, dear ones.

What will come to pass in the coming days will amaze and astonish you. Keep your faith; keep the lamp of faith within well-lit. For as you journey to these other worlds, you will no longer be the teacher, the sage, but also the student in these coming days.

For all has been foretold in the ancient books of lore, the turning of the masses toward the heavenly skies, and all before you will be revealed the lies. Some may astonish more than most, but still, your eyes will settle on the heavenly host of angels that appear to you now, surrounding you and uplifting you into their love and light, and there you will sit in the midst of it and yet it will feel as if you are separated from it – like watching a movie while surrounded by blessed family and friends knowing it will all come to an end – the drama, the stage, the final chess play. All have been designed for the highest reaction this time.

And yet, so many of you will not react. Almost as if it cannot touch you anymore, for you are no longer a part of the 3D reality. And although you stand there, you know you are standing in other worlds as well, and this is just the latest imagining come-to-play show and tell.

So let your spirits soar high, allow the final showdown to show itself to the world, and know just around the corner is the new beginning you have been hoping for. Know that as things get to looking really bad, it is just this – a fractional reality at best, and it is all finally coming to an end. Clearing the stage for the brand new play, a life of your wildest imaginings coming into sight – the arrival is just in time.

So get out of your own way this time. Allow the heavenly angels to beam their loving light. Allow the earthly sojourn to bask and bathe and absorb the everlasting streams of light weaving brand new patterns into your hearts and minds.

And know this; it is about time. A long journey you have weathered, and you are still alive. It is time to rejoice, dearest children of mine; it is time to put away the swords and allow the Creator's light to find you this time.

Do not fear, although you might, stay focused on building a brand new way of life, and above all else, rise above your fear and hold the light – hold the light as it is your lifeline.

Confusion to end and a new age to begin – the Age of Aquarius is coming in.

With love, light, and blessings to all of you, dearest Children of the Light – warmest of blessings to all of you, my Divine and Heavenly Tribe – for you are all dearest children of mine.

I AM Your Mother Divine showering you with blessings of heavenly light.

What does this message mean to you?

What action or feelings does this inspire in you?

How can you bring the wisdom of this message into your daily life?

Hold the Light of Unconditional Love

Holy angels of the heavenly light – hold onto your faith, dearest children of mine. Hold the light of a Mother's divine love. Unconditional. Full of grace and hope.

For that is what I wish for you, dear ones. I wish for you a loving light to see you through hard times. I wish for you a blazing fire to burn away the fear and negativity you encounter. I wish you safe travels, and I welcome you home.

For a mother's heart is never alone. I bathe you in my power and light. I uplift you in the evening light. I embrace you in each new day to come, and I want you to know you are brighter and braver than I ever could have hoped.

For in each passing moment in time, in this play called life, I wish for you more joy than you have ever known. I wish for you not to feel alone. During the panic and the sad times, know that it is just a blip on this screen called life.

Know that you are more than you could ever imagine and that the stars that blink at night glow brighter and steadier in the darkened night. Never to be extinguished, never to stop sharing their heavenly gifts - the journey to the manger of the 3 wise men. A guiding light, a beacon of hope, the star of Bethlehem returning you to the heart of love, the peace of joy, the journey of an everlasting glimmer of my own Divine light. Showing itself to you one at a time until all behold the holiness of the December sky - the turning point of one age to another, a ripple in the fabric of life, a momentous miracle about to take place and witnessed by the human race.

With love in our hearts and hope in our light, we send you great blessings, dearest children of mine.

Keep on holding your very bright lights, keep on shining, and staying safe – we wish for you to know how sacred you are, we wish for you to know we see you as our stars – for where we sit, we ponder at night, as we gaze upon the earth with our loving minds, we see you all lit up like you see the stars in your sky we see you as holy and wise. Our gift to humanity is that you internalize the significant majesty you are in your own eyes.

Many blessings to you, dearest hearts of light. May love to envelop and embrace you – for you are all Divine. For you are all dearest children of mine.

Blessings, dear children, until the morning light. Mother Mary and the Legions of Light

THE REBIRTH OF HEAVEN ON EARTH

What does this message mean to you?

What action or feelings does this inspire in you?

How can you bring the wisdom of this message into your daily life?

The New Dimension is Now in Sight

Holy children of the light – the new dimension is now in sight. Step forward, one step at a time to your brand new life. The light is shining from within each of you. What will you create when you are able to see the new vision of light? Rainbow colors you have never seen before will flow before you in bubbles of peace and love. Refracted fragments of the world you have come from will return in due time, but only those that you allow into your lives.

For each one of you is a creation made new. In each one of you, God's light is shining brighter than ever before, although the majesty we see in you, you are just beginning to explore. A wealth of higher energy is flowing in and through and all around you now. We are beckoning the beacons of heaven on earth to step forward to help you now. Reach for the pillars of light you sense in front of you and allow the columns of precious energy to surround you / infuse you with the majestic colors, sights, and sounds of the heavenly realms.

Rest. Breathe. Bring in the state of peace.

Infuse your energy, absorb with each breath you take a higher level of awareness, of sensory perception that awakens a profound knowing deep inside of you – that you were meant to build worlds with your imaginations, dear ones. You have the power inside you if you let it out now.

Flow forth from you a burst of colors of new sights and sounds; imagine what you want your world to look like now – in the newness and grace bestowed upon you, dear souls, it is a moment in creation to brighten your lights and create a heavenly life. Nothing is out of the picture. All is possible if you let it.

Stay positive. Stay focused.

Create the new world from deep inside your soul, infuse it with the love of your higher heart center, and raise it up into your conscious creation.

Rest. Allow.

Breathe it in now. The sights, the colors, the sounds. All is new. All are waiting for you.

It is done. We are all one.

Bless you, dearest children of light, for creating what is now in sight.

Allow your hearts to rejoice in mine. Loving light of Creator's sanctuary of love.

Blessings, dear ones.

I AM the Beacon of Hope. You will meet me when you step over the threshold. Hearts and hands in mine. Together we will travel to a new lifetime.

Mother Divine and the Legions of Light

What does this message mean to you?

What action or feelings does this inspire in you?

How can you bring the wisdom of this message into your daily life?

Allow Your Soul to Blossom, Bloom, and Grow

Dearest children of the heavenly light – you are awakening a little at a time, a little more every day, every time you raise your hearts and hands to heaven and allow us to fill you with our love.

For you are, each of you, a divine blessing, and we are so heartened to see so many in prayer – so many relieving themselves of worldly desires, possessions, and tasks at hand to set aside their hearts in prayer.

So many praying for the good of all – so many reaching out and lending a hand instead of going to the mall.

This heartens us to see the soul of humanity healing so well. It has been a long time coming in your earthly years, and yet

THE REBIRTH OF HEAVEN ON EARTH

we knew you would always get here - to this place and time where your worthiness starts to shine and the heavens, the stars, backlight the light shining from the inner depths - bringing peace, love, and happiness.

For the journey has been long and hard, and yet there have been so many moments of pure triumph.

We would like to say - keep on keeping on, but at this time, we send much love to shore up your reserves and to keep you in our midst, for we see you moving great distance in an instant you are across the bridge into the heavenly realms, the realms of heaven on earth that have been laid before you - you are in the final stages of the crossing dear ones, the last steps to take before you are swept into a brand new place.

So take a deep breath, allow your souls to blossom, bloom, and grow and carry you buoyantly the rest of the way home.

THE REBIRTH OF HEAVEN ON EARTH

We are waiting for you - a welcoming party of heavenly hosts, and we embrace you and hold you until you glow, smiling and laughing from the depths of your souls.

Blessings, dear ones - your Heavenly Hosts

What does this message mean to you?

What action or feelings does this inspire in you?

How can you bring the wisdom of this message into your daily life?

Uncover the Magic that is about to Unfold

Heavenly child of the earthly light – we are waking in you much desire to create, to move, to censor the impulses within that are calling to you to stand down, stay down, sit down, and yet you are awakening even more as you let go of the voices telling you to do that. The more those voices within the call to tell you that you are weak, the more they threaten defeat, the more something else more deep awakens and enlivens you and shores up your reserves, for the journey is not yet over, dear one.

For you are just beginning to delve into the depths of your soul – to uncover the magic that is just on the cusp, right about to unfold.

Journey deep within, uncovering greater depth with each breath you take, allowing the other voices, those of doubt, to wash away – allow your soul to be rinsed clean, and then, continue to breathe and this time breathe in – clouds of light fluffy and bright filling the spaces like cotton candy, pink and sweet, the stuff of which dreams are made. And sit and rest in the soft stillness for a moment before your next breath, and when you take it allow it to fill you even deeper, even more, until the fluffy white stillness surrounds you at your core, then work your way out, with this substance of love, and allow your heart to beat at an increasingly steady pace, as you open the doorway to a symphony of sights and sounds, the heart of the universe dancing around; light and free, blessed and caressed, a beacon of joy, love, and happiness.

We come to you from the infinite light of holiness in grace and loving tides – to wash you, to cleanse you of the debris you have absorbed from the negativity and loneliness and all sorts of the scourge. Take our hands as we lead you away from the area of bathing into the spa-like fragrance of jasmine, and then breathe in – deep – again. Find your lounge – be it a chair or a chaise – and take sweet fragrance in your embrace. Allow your sorrows, your fears, to simply be washed away. Today is the day to rest and play. No more worries, no more stress. All are surrounded by the love of peace, joy, and happiness.

Peace, now the dearest child of light – this is a rest stop along the rail of life.

Take your time.

Rest. Play.

Allow yourself to just give way.

We've got you, holding you tight, our wings wrapped around you in a blanket of peace and light.

THE REBIRTH OF HEAVEN ON EARTH

No worries. No stress.

Simply rest on a blanket of happiness.

Soon you will journey to the next phase after the sorrows have been washed away.

There you will re-learn how to dance and play. Light-hearted, sure-footed to journey the rest of the way.

For now, just rest, at least for one more day.

The lamps have been lit, and the path shines before you, with a twinkling of stars sprinkled for pure delight along the way.

For now, just rest, at least for one more day.

THE REBIRTH OF HEAVEN ON EARTH

Welcoming you home into the inner sanctum of your divine and sacred life.

Penelope and the Angels of De-Light

What does this message mean to you?

What action or feelings does this inspire in you?

How can you bring the wisdom of this message into your daily life?

Honor the Cycle of Clearing and Healing

Holy child – Your heart has been weary and tired, and we see you are clearing out so much debris, so much of the old hurts and dis-ease. This has made you sad and angry and without hope, but we wish to tell you that this is just a passing phase, this clearing out. It is important for you to honor this cycle of clearing, of healing, for much is not as it appears, dear one.

For the clearing has to occur before you can welcome the season in the sun.

For light to appear in the darkest of corners, dear, first, the darkness needs to clear.

THE REBIRTH OF HEAVEN ON EARTH

Once you have released all that you no longer need, your spirit is freed to welcome in more light, more love, and more blessings, dear one.

This has been a difficult lesson for you to learn.

Rest, dear one.

For it has been a long haul.

Rest, dear one.

And let go of all that needs to go. Let it go. No need to hold onto it any longer.

Breathe and release.

Let go of all dis-ease.

Trust.

Hope.

Allow each breath to welcome in more light.

Allow each breath to carry you closer to home, to the joy you were born to create, to the serenity you were born to bathe in and breathe, and each time you breathe, you come closer again to the person you were always meant to be, to the soul of the heavens that is residing within you – to the holy spirit that brings grace and a new opportunity to heal and rejoice and be at peace.

Be still and watch the world turn around you.

Do not engage in the drama that unfolds.

Simply observe and hold your own – your center, dear child. And continue to go within and observe the microcosm inside of you that is being reflected in the outer world around you. And heal what needs to be healed deep within until each day begins again. And continue to breathe, continue to reflect, until you start to enjoy what comes next until you appreciate what the outer world reflects. And then you will be surrounded by all that befriends, all that welcomes you in. And you will enjoy the world you are participating, actively creating, in.

Be in joy. Be in peace. Be in love. And soon, you will see the world reflecting these qualities back to you, dear one. But first, you must release what no longer serves and welcome in the light and the blessings, the healing you so deserve.

For we can send you healing, we can send you blessings, but these you must absorb. You must allow it. You must draw it in and see what you need to cleanse.

This is a period of cleansing. And you will see evidence of this as you begin to heal. You will see the cleansing occurring in the outer world as well. Do not be afraid. This is how healing occurs. First, the wounds rise to the surface in order to be heard (seen or witnessed), dear friend. Then the clearing and the healing can begin.

You are at a brave turning point. Do not be afraid. Allow the healing to wash over you in waves with every breath you take.

And you will be saved by everlasting Grace.

Rest and be at peace during this final stage of healing; the final stage of clearing takes place.

We are the Angels of Heaven, and you are safe in our embrace.

What does this message mean to you?

What action or feelings does this inspire in you?

How can you bring the wisdom of this message into your daily life?

The Clouds have Disappeared

Holy children of the light – your hearts are breaking open and cleansing of all darkness at this time.

What awaits you after this period of cleansing is a heart full of light, full of triumph, full of joy.

For that is what makes stars shine, the absence of darkness in their blazing and holy light, and that is how you are meant to shine. No more dark and damp shadows clinging to the vine. All is one in holy light.

All are aware of the light of the Creator that shines through – the clouds have disappeared, and all that is left is what is truly you, holy and true. The brightness and the brilliance are awaiting you.

THE REBIRTH OF HEAVEN ON EARTH

For you have burned off all the dross.

Let go of all that you are not.

And in the midst of the shadows, you have found what is truly you.

And you are shining now – breaking through the darkness and emerging into the world of light.

A world of divine purpose, the passion to create a beautiful life, not only for yourself but for those around you who are still wandering and wondering in the darkness, and to them, you will shine your light and be an ever-lasting guide.

For you have traveled many millions of miles not only in this short life but in numerous lifetimes – so many roles you have played in this stage of this time, and yet you have emerged effervescent and full of divine light, and so you will show others who come to you how to traverse their most recent roles, how to conquer the challenges and emerge into the oneness just like you.

For they may need teachers who have been through this thing called life, those who can relate to them on the level they are at and show them how to weave their way through the challenges that present themselves just like the angels have shown you.

For you will become the angel in human form, and you will become the teachers you all wished you could have learned from.

For we have done our part, but for you, the forebearers, the journey was quite hard – for you had to believe, you had to trust when others could not sense or accept the gifts you possessed or the inclination to follow your own happiness. The world has changed so much since then, and yet, the journey continues for those on the path, the path to oneness, to light, to love, and then to discover the gifts that lay dormant within them.

For each of you has a spark of the divine. Each of you has a gift to give during this lifetime. And that is what you are always searching for, are you not?

For your passion, your purpose, the gifts you need to impart? And so you shall discover more of your innate and dormant magic, the crystalline essence of your love and your light, and you shall give more than you shall take, and you shall live a much longer time than those who came before you, for this time, in this life, you shall have discovered your connection to the divine – you shall discover the source and the power of the light that shines within and never again shall you forget your place in the universe dear children.

Never again shall you despair.

Never again shall you feel separate and alone, for you will know the power of your own heart and what sets the world aglow.

And then you will show the others, and they too will come to know themselves as great warriors of wisdom and light, and the world will become a great beacon, shining and bright, and the universe will rejoice in the journey that took place.

For Mother Divine and her children to once again join the human race, the brethren from outer space. One family united in love, passion, and purpose to recover their station and their integration with the light that shines as the source of all that is, and the world will become free and holy once again.

The Masters of Grace and the Holiness within the Human Race. St. Paul and the Colossians – Soon, you shall be free.

What does this message mean to you?

What action or feelings does this inspire in you?

How can you bring the wisdom of this message into your daily life?

Emerging from the Cocoon

Holy children, angels of light – We are watching you shine amidst the darkness of the current tide.

For though your lives seem bleak, sequestered, and silenced, so to speak, you are still so much shining light – you are still so much more loving than in past times. You are emerging from the cocoons, and soon you shall walk forward in peace, love, joy, and appreciation for all that has transpired.

For you are healing despite all the setbacks you have seen in the past year, you are still moving forward. Many of you have used the time to heal emotional and physical wounds – still, so many of you are clearing from the darkness you have absorbed.

For the gift of this past year has been time – has it not? Time to reflect, to stop all the nonsense and the noise that previously kept you 'going' all the time. And though time is not a reality in many dimensions, it is a primary construct of yours, and so time is important for you to absorb in silence; new learnings, new relationships, new insight on all that has surrounded you for so much of your lifetimes. Finally, you can sit and rest.

And for those of you who have experienced more than your fair share of turmoil, dis-ease, and unrest – you still have had time to wonder and reflect. What does this all mean? Where are we, really? Is there really such a thing as varying dimensions, varying versions of reality? Is this just a dream? How can I make my life more important and filled with more meaning? Look at all this suffering; the world has to get better than this, and we cannot stay in a place like this.

And so, whatever your path, you have set off to greener pastures, a new land of creation where you are manifesting so quickly whatever you desire. So watch your thoughts and keep your eyes on the prize, full of hope and patience and be wise. Set your sights on not what has passed but what is coming in, dear children, at last.

For this is the dawning of a new creation in time. The thoughts and prayers of all of you are now being made manifest, although you cannot see it yet - most of you can sense that change is in the air. So settle in for the turning of the tide, settle in, and let your spirit rise in hope and faith that all has not been for naught. In fact, all have already risen to the top - lying in wait just across the horizon to be welcomed in from just the right spot.

All are waiting for you. Heaven on Earth. That is what is waiting to be born.

So take a deep breath and know that change is here, welcome in the changing tide and learn to rise above the waves of fear, knowing that heaven on earth is dawning, my dears.

In love, light, and blessings from my light to yours – igniting the flame of forgiveness in all those hearts of yours.

For I AM Your Mother, Your Mother Divine, and you are ALL blessed children of mine.

What does this message mean to you?

What action or feelings does this inspire in you?

How can you bring the wisdom of this message into your daily life?

Living in a Virtual Reality

Dearest child of light – Opening your heart and mind. All is not as it appears in the outer world, dear child. All are arranged for maximum capacity / maximum density / maximum opening of hearts and minds. For the collective are still asleep, dear child. Many do not know the magical essence of what is all around them, dear child. For all the angels, masters, and guides helping them through this experience / this illusion / this 'game' called life.

For all are not real. All are make-believe. All you have to do to shift your reality is to make real what you want to create. All are imagined, dear child. A figment of your imagination, a reality set on a tv screen that is invisible but all around you, dear child. Every moment you breathe, you are creating what you shall see. The feeling is the connection between you and me. Feeling allows you to break free. Your heart is your anchor between dimensions, the conduit through which you experience what you create. The mind sees, the heart feels, and the ears hear.

Move into your senses – feel more than you see, sense more than you see, hear within your mind's eye and not with your ears, dear child. There is a whole world teeming around you that you are unaware of, dear child. It is time to move into this other world, to shift what you are experiencing on a daily basis. It is time for you to expand your consciousness beyond this dimension – move out of the fear, out of the experiences that you hear, that you see and listen to every night on the big screens – remove yourself from those experiences, go within and sense a whole new world you can enter, a whole new world just waiting for you to step in and begin again.

Stop. Rest.

Move forward by going within.

Sense and feel this new group energy, the angels and guides that are around you at all times.

Ask them to guide you. Ask them to take you by the hand and lead you the rest of the way.

It is time to build a brand new way of life, a brand new creation happening from the inside. All is possible now, dear child. NO limitations. Unleash the ties that bind you to the reality you see at this time. It is not real at all, dear child. It is an imagining of fear that have you beguiled. Bewitched. Bemused. In fear. It is up to you to unwind and extract your controlling mind.

Step inside.

To this new dimension you hold in your heart and mind, deep inside, you know the time has come for this play to the end and for you to begin again, right where you stand, but again – a brand new life, you decide who you want to be and that will set you free. You are a free agent. You can do and be anything you decide. This is a beginning of a brand-new lifetime.

Be holy. Be wise. Blessings to you where you reside.

> *Blessings to you, dearest children of light, for I AM Your Mother Divine, and you are all blessed children of mine.*

THE REBIRTH OF HEAVEN ON EARTH

What does this message mean to you?

What action or feelings does this inspire in you?

How can you bring the wisdom of this message into your daily life?

Breathe Healing into the World

Dearest child of the heavenly light – Life, Love, Liberty, All of the blessings of heaven and earth surround you in the ether world, dear ones.

For all that you have asked for is here; you only need to draw it near.

Breathe in, dear child, all of the anxieties of the world you wish to quell – and release them now fully transformed and healed by the breath of the angels you hold inside of you.

Breathe this healing out into the world, for you are a conduit of the heavenly soul, and the breath of your soul speaks volumes, dear child. The breath of your soul is sacred and pure, release its power and send it forth to walk before you wherever you may go – to soothe others with the healing power of your most powerful soul.

The sun that shines before you is nothing more than a reflection of the power you hold. Deep inside, the power is waiting to be unleashed onto the heavenly realms, being built in the ether world and healing, transformed by the power of your own soul.

Set your intentions upon the world.

Light it up with the power of your breath, the power of your intent.

Let go of the rest.

Never mind the stories that you hear on the evening news, the cryptic messages streaming at you, the corruption and evil that you see around you – that is all made up by you, that is an illusion of the outer world; start to live by the truth you see within yourself / within your soul, and you will birth multitudes of tremendous change all around you.

The truth of the world is born within you.

Release and let it go, your soul moving forward out into the world.

Blessings shall fall upon you as you do.

Spheres of golden light surround you, wrapping you in the golden embrace of these magical and holy spheres of love, blessing you with the Creator's light and wrapping you in His sweet embrace, giving you the honor of embracing your own creations, your own inner light / your own inner life.

For what is born inside you now is brought to life. Holy, sacred, your inner truth – making the outer world truly a reflection of the truths you hold inside of you. Like a painter with a brush, make the colors those of love.

For you are truly sacred dear ones.

> *For I AM Your Mother Divine, and you are ALL blessed children of heavenly light.*
>
> *Sacred and free, breathing new life into Thee.*
>
> *Amen, and Blessed Be.*

THE REBIRTH OF HEAVEN ON EARTH

What does this message mean to you?

What action or feelings does this inspire in you?

How can you bring the wisdom of this message into your daily life?

On the Precipice of the Great Return

Holy angels breathe in the light of new life. For in your path is an opening taking place, a pathway to the higher dimensions through the inner sanctum of your hearts is opening up.

Can you feel the easier, lighter energy as you breathe this new light in?

Can you feel the way your joy is returning, dearest children?

For we are on the precipice of the great return – a return to love and the ways of love that have been forgone for many millennia, dearest ones.

For you are each a light in the path of darkness, and together with the realms of illumined truth, you have begun the return to the place we call home – the heavenly realms deep within you. And along your journey, you have become aware of the place within the inner earth and those who reside there.

For the earth is not unlike each of you; she has an inner sanctum where life thrives and where it is filled with comfort and peace and great adventures to take place. Deep within her, as within each of you, there is an inner sanctum filled with higher wisdom, brighter light, and joyfulness that embraces all humankind. And it is from such place, such a state deep within, that all of the universes are connected and lit up once again. As the fires burn from the holy light, new life is born into the ethers beyond all periods of space and time, and it is from here that you can create whatever is your dream, whatever it is you wish to see in the outer reality.

For first, creation is born in the inner world's dearest child of mine, and then it moves into the ethers, where it is stored until there is enough energy for the return to outer form.

Now your creations are resting in the ethers; you have taken the time to foster your dreams, you have created new thought forms and new energies, and now it is time for you to breathe, to relax into the creation of your dreams.

As you relax and rejoice, the opening appears, and one by one or in a flash from above, what is waiting in the ethers appears in pure form, and all of the world is suddenly reborn.

The tired old stage disappears from your life, and all that remains is pure and heavenly light.

THE REBIRTH OF HEAVEN ON EARTH

This is how the dawning of the age of desire, the age of peace and love and joy, is birthed, and the Kali Yuga turns into the age of Aquarius. One at a time, you shall come, each in your own state of readiness, as within so as above.

Lessons learned, freedom is hard won, and thoughtfully each of you shall emerge & merge into one. One heavenly body of love and warmth, embracing each other and yourselves – walking hand in hand into the lessons of love, walking as one light into the heavenly realms residing right here on earth, and embracing the love of God, which is yours.

Walk with the angels of the higher mind, the heart-mind, and there you shall find the keys to the gates of heaven are open; walk with determination and fierceness in love, and your hearts will open into the stage of peace, joy, and love.

THE REBIRTH OF HEAVEN ON EARTH

Creations of the inner dimensions are shown forth in the spirit of grace from above.

We are in the dimension of unconditional love.

Bear witness to the testimony of the birth of the new earth. Judge not. Simply walk forward and embrace it all from the depths of your own inner hearts.

Blessings, dear ones, welcome into the heart of love, the heart of the universe, for together, we all walk as one.

I AM your Mother Divine, and you are all heavenly children of mine.

THE REBIRTH OF HEAVEN ON EARTH

What does this message mean to you?

What action or feelings does this inspire in you?

How can you bring the wisdom of this message into your daily life?

Speak Your Truth and Rejoice

Holy children of the heavenly light - we are rejoicing with you in the inner planes of de-light, for wisdom is yours, hard-won and well-fought. The journey to the light within your soul has been happening whether you are aware of it or not. For now, you have forsaken all that has come before.

Now is the time to step forward.

Speak your truth, dear beacons of love - placing your full hearts forward to rejoice in the new meaning of glorious love.

For no more will there be shadows everywhere you turn. No more will there be shadows covering your hearts.

For you will be able to move forward, breathing more deeply, sighing in peace, and surrounded by angels on your journey.

Even if it seems there are more cobwebs to clear out, that darkness still abounds; know these dearest children of love – all of the shadows are on their way out, to be replaced by unicorns and rainbows, not all at once but in waves of ever-increasing inclinations of light – one sacred heart opening at a time.

You have crossed the divide, dearest children of mine, and I am holding you safe on 'the other side' – merely a fraction of a degree of heavenly light yet separate and apart from the chaos you used to find.

Allow your hearts to settle into mine.

THE REBIRTH OF HEAVEN ON EARTH

Allow your hands to be held and embraced in the name of love.

And allow the heavenly messengers to send you our words of comfort and healing, and allow the rest of the world to burst forth in the flowers of Spring.

The welcoming, the embrace of the human angelic race.

It is time, dearest children of mine.

Time to hold the new line. To draw a line in the sand to whence you will never go back and to move endlessly forward toward the sacred space in between, the land of your heart, the land of your dreams.

For you have journeyed far and wide, so many experiences – you had to decide, and yet you did, you imagined it, you rejoiced in it, and now you will experience it - the land / the life you have held deep inside for so many lifetimes. Visions of Lemuria, Atlantis of the Highest Age, so many civilizations where you tried to reach this stage - and yet you are here, you have succeeded, you have gone deep within and routed out the dis-ease, you kept journeying deep inside your soul, you kept moving through it all - the tragedy, the suffering - you do not need it anymore. Now you are standing in a brand new place, a brand new stage, and though it may look the same, it is infinitely more pleasing to you - the coming of age to the brilliance of your own hearts and minds, to your own inner light.

Rejoice, dearest children of mine - for I am the Mother of All Life, and I have been waiting to embrace you, to hold you close, and for you to remember me this time.

Blessings, dearest children of light – for you are the beacons of hope for the others following behind. I AM Your Mother, and You are Mine.

Blessings from your Mother Divine.

What does this message mean to you?

What action or feelings does this inspire in you?

How can you bring the wisdom of this message into your daily life?

Infinite Possibilities Surround You Now

Holy children of the heavenly light - the realms of infinity, of infinite possibilities, surround you at this time.

For you have risen into the higher vibrations, and new worlds are opening up as a result of your imagination.

Let go of all that is passed.

For it no longer exists, for you are walking on a completely fresh/new path - one filled with golden light and an infinite embrace of heavenly delights.

And we are so proud of you, dearest children of love.

For keeping your circumstance away from your creativity and your perseverance for the betterment of lots.

THE REBIRTH OF HEAVEN ON EARTH

For deep in your angelic hearts, you rose to the occasion and uncovered the strength you have always known, and the wisdom deep inside you has kept you moving forward.

For there is nowhere to go but up, of course!

And we are waiting with you, pushing you, holding your hands, and watching you / cheering you on as you journey into new lands built from your imaginations.

You have truly become the creators of your own destinies, and if you cannot feel it, sense it, or see it yet, know that we do – we can feel it, see it, and sense it, and it is born from your own inner magnificence, all of it, in all your glory, and it is even more than you imagined it would be, and you will walk freely and happily into the sacred space of this new and holy place.

For you are holy, and you deserve to live peacefully and joyfully and know that you will, you are, and you will experience the beauty of all that you are already, all that you already have separate from what appears as your 'current circumstance.'

Wipe away the illusions and keep the rose-colored glasses on, for what you are about to encounter will blow even those magical glasses off – that's how magnificent you all are, and the new worlds that have been created are even more blessed than your conscious imaginations will allow – just allow, just be, just create and allow the new stage to settle in and take place.

For you are magnificent and holy beacons of love, of light, you are the Creator's imagination come to life, and you will continue to create new and better worlds throughout your life, and your experience will begin to reflect this new state of mind. Holiness, dearest children of mine. Holiness and sacredness of all life – that is what is now coming into the light, into your lives.

Blessings, dearest children of mine, for I AM Your Mother, and You Are ALL Divine!

What does this message mean to you?

What action or feelings does this inspire in you?

How can you bring the wisdom of this message into your daily life?

The Sacred Script of Your Brand New Life

Child of bright wonder and de-light, such a dreamer with such keen insight. You are not all gathered up in the clouds, simply getting ready for the world of your dreams to come to you now. You have waited so long with your heart on the shelf. Time to come full circle back to your most holy self. Your true self, a soldier of the light, the heartwarming smile, a heavenly sight. Your Mother and I are standing by your side. No longer the divide. A true family – the holy trinity – is now inside your heart and mind.

Holy, holy, holy, sacred, and free, blessed life is calling to thee.

Take me along for the ride, not just your Mother but your Father, Divine. This is the sacred script of your brand-new life. All-inclusive trip – open your heart, open it wide. Find the love that is bound inside.

Release and let go of the troubles of the past. Release and move forward into the new dimensions at last.

You can have the wisdom of your dreams, the light in your life so much larger than it seems. Your joy and your wonder will be the birth of new light.; traveling in store, no more struggle and strife.

Welcoming you, the dearest heart of mine, into the wisdom of your holy sight.

Allow your mind to wander, your heart is torn asunder, into the newness – let go of the past; this was a life never meant to last. Lasted so much longer than was planned.

THE REBIRTH OF HEAVEN ON EARTH

This is a new beginning – a new stage – a new calling coming your way.

Time to play a brand new play. So much joy and laughter – get out of the way and let us set up the stage.

Holy rejoicing reminiscent of lifetimes past – lessons long passed – now in the doorway of the dreams that you seek/see newness in everything / every living thing.

You are our daughter – born from great love, the light of the future is in your heart and your soul – allow them to become one dear one we call to you out of love. Rest in the knowing, and you are well taken care of.

> *Your Father in Heaven is calling to you, dearest child, the heart of the wanderer/wanderer – sit, rest, smile, for we have been with you all the while.*

What does this message mean to you?

What action or feelings does this inspire in you?

How can you bring the wisdom of this message into your daily life?

THE REBIRTH OF HEAVEN ON EARTH

Life is Not a War to be Fought

Holy children of the heavenly realms – here you reside on earth all upside down.

For what you believe is about to turn full circle, truths to be laid out from what has been happening underground. And the full truth you may never be allowed to know, but there are soldiers of the light helping you now.

Focus not on what has happened in the past, the behind-the-scenes machinations and strategies.

For the past no longer belongs to you now. It never happened from what you know in the 'now.'

This is all make-believe, my dear friends. It is all a construct of your imagination. Move forward now into another dream, breaking from the illusion that you have created, where monsters and myths take place no more. No more space in your heart, your body, or your mind, dearest children of mine.

For I Am Your Mother Divine, and it is in the quickening that you realize there is no such thing as time. There is no such thing as reality unless you choose to make it your reality in your own heart and mind. So only allow the loving thoughts to abide, to take up space in your hearts and minds.

For when there is nothing but sunshine on the inside, then you will real-ize (make real) only that which your hearts desire.

For never in your imagination did you create such horrid dreams as the truths that come out would make it seem. And then it depends on who you are talking to – which story you wish to believe. They are all lies, dearest ones, and your truth, as it seems, is based on which lies you choose to believe. There is not only one story. Each of you creates the story – creates the lesson and the joy or the sorrow you wish to experience at any moment.

Allow yourselves the luxury of observing as if watching the grandest of plays, the most sacred mystery about to take center stage.

The magic and the wonder – the joy on your face, as you real-ize this is not what you wanted to create and the knowing that you can choose to create another story, another play. Just as you are watching a gory horror story on your TV, when the story gets to you too much, you are free to stand up and change the channel or simply change your reality with the flick of the remote. You are seeing a new scene, something very serene. The nature channel, a meditation journey, floating on waves of joyful vibrations – it is that easy. Taking control of your mind as if it was a TV screen, what type of story do you wish to see?

Envision it in order to make it your real-ity / your own real-ity TV screen.

Allow the scenes to play before you and take it all to some degree, only that what you wish to experience comes into your personal screen, building a wall or fence a lining perhaps so that you only take in what you want to give space to. You would not welcome a serial killer into your home, would you? Then why would you welcome them into your TV set? The screen should be the only that you wish to see in your own vibratory reality.

Focus on that.

Meditate on the meaning of that.

You control your senses, and your real-ity is simply mirroring the vibration you have allowed to seep/sneak in. There are many ways of controlling your dear children. The first starts with permeating the field around you. The second comes from the willingness inside of you. Both need to be in harmony or conflict but never are they to stand inside you – you are separate, and yet you are all one – the vibration around you influences you too, dear ones.

Surround yourself in clean and pleasant eye-catching, uplifting harmonious places, and soon you will see serenity on your sweet faces.

Allow your soul to be battered and torn, and soon you will find more ways to cry, dear ones. It is that simple.

Allow your life to take flight by bringing in more light – through prayer, meditation, joyful fun, and laughter, dear ones.

Life is not a war to be won.

Yes, you heard that right – Life is not a war to be won.

Life is a pleasant journey if you allow it, dear ones.

Here is the hard truth – all you have been taught is about to go 'poof' / 'boom,' and all that is left is the bounty of your imagination.

Let your vibration clear from all the negative patterns.

Let it all go, all that you think you know – about wars and natural disasters, about the vaccine and the pandemic, and all of the other dis-ease in your world. This is not the world you were brought into – this is the world that has been contaminated by negative vibrations. It is not real dear ones. It is not real unless you let it be, dear ones.

Lift yourselves up into a higher place, a more beautiful stage, a more positive play.

Rise up into the higher visions of reality, the higher dimensions, the more sacred place where you can roam free and create a new reality. This is only a journey. We see what we want to see.

What do you want to believe?

What do you want to create?

Focus only on that and let go of the rest.

THE REBIRTH OF HEAVEN ON EARTH

The trouble and turmoil will dissolve when you allow them to rest.

Breathe life into your new reality – focus on the pretty, the easy, and the joy-fulfilling prophecies. The rest is full of dis-ease; the attention you give it does nothing to please, and only causes more irony/agony.

Let go of the dis-ease, and soon you will see a bright horizon beyond the existing galaxy, a bright and sunny stargazing experience that will lift all of your senses.

Take comfort in knowing this; all that sits before you no longer exists. It happened a million light years ago – you are only now witnessing it.

Rest and be blessed. This is an old story no longer playing out. It is time to let go of it. You are watching the past disintegrate before your eyes, nothing more, nothing less. Focus on what brings you happiness.

Dearest child, just rest.

Let it float away on the breeze.

Realize you can create the life you dream of.

Dream well, dearest hearts of sunshine, dream well and release the paradigm that is old and ending, be freed from the illusions of fear and doubt – the world has become something brand new, and so my dears, it will be reflected inside and outside of you, the way you see the world will bring new blessings to you.

THE REBIRTH OF HEAVEN ON EARTH

Continue to believe in what brings you comfort and joy, and release the rest, do not hit rewind, but fast forward into the bright sunshine.

With love and blessings from the heart of Mother Divine to you, my dear children, creators of new life/light.

What does this message mean to you?

What action or feelings does this inspire in you?

How can you bring the wisdom of this message into your daily life?

The Curve has been Turned

Holy child of light – this is a message for humanity, for change is in sight. The curve has been turned, lessons well-worn, and now the healing has begun.

For there are many that still do not understand what has been happening in the higher realms.

For many do not yet understand what they have come here to do. The troubles and turmoil of the everyday world you see in front of you have clouded their vision and left them confused.

For many, there are days of healing old emotional wounds, and for others, the journey has already started of moving into the higher realms.

For all, the tables have turned. The lessons are just beginning for some.

For those of you that have had a hard time of late, that is because you are entering the final stage of ascension – you are just on the cusp of entering the new world you have created for yourselves. The door has opened, and you are in the middle of the doorway, moving across the threshold. There are some more bumps coming, it may be a rocky ride, but the final push is right on the other side. The doors are opened, and the light is shining bright. Enjoy the fresh air, the crystals that breathe and send you more light – the bounty of heaven just beyond your senses – all of it surrounding you and bathing you in a magical embrace, the love of God entering your space.

For you have, indeed, not really gone anywhere – your feet still touch the ground, you still breathe in Earth's atmosphere, and yet you have entered into a new space and time, a sphere of magical possibilities surrounds and embraces you, and you are in your own little bubble of magical space, a space of infinite possibilities as you learn to co-create.

How will you decorate?

How will you allow your space to breathe and embrace this new energy?

For this is a vibrant, new, living energy that moves with you and raises you into the higher dimensions of the reality you choose to create.

You may not feel any different – and yet, there is a lightness to your step and ease or element of grace that fills you up so that you are no longer affected by the 'rules of the road' and the lessons of the lower dimensions, the 3D and 4D realms of existence. This is what it means to 'transcend' – to 'rise above' and create a world that serves you, dear child.

To serve you not in a selfish way – for the needs of materiality have mostly been complete. Your needs will encompass those of greater humanity, for your vision of what you want to create, has expanded beyond your current limitations.

All possibilities are now on the table.

Choose what you like and leave the rest.

All are designed for greater levels of happiness.

Just rest.

THE REBIRTH OF HEAVEN ON EARTH

For the journey has been exhausting, we see.

For you have journeyed farther than any in the history of humanity. And though your history may be so much longer than you are aware, still this journey has been the most taxing and emotionally charged with the purging of all that has come before.

And now, you must rest as you let go and allow yourself to be carried over the final step of the divine threshold – enveloped in the love and light of another world, one you have dreamed of often and sometimes visited in your sleep, but now your journey is becoming complete.

The ups and downs and turbulence will eventually abate, and you will know that you are truly safe.

THE REBIRTH OF HEAVEN ON EARTH

Safe enough to create love and peace and harmony and blessings for all.

We are the Council of Light connecting with you all.

What does this message mean to you?

What action or feelings does this inspire in you?

How can you bring the wisdom of this message into your daily life?

The Slate is Wiped Clean

Holy child of heavenly light, there are many who surround you at this time - many from the heavenly realm looking upon you with loving intention, waiting for the embrace of the Starseed nations. Wholesome and clean, this world is not as it seems, and yet, we see so much clearing of unwanted pain. The years have gone by in a flash, and yet still, so many of you are holding onto the past. The pain, the dis-ease - washed away in the breeze. So many truths are rising to the surface - to uncover and heal the pains of the past, and yet you are already walking in truth way past that. The old becomes new once the roadways have cleared - the lessons of your ancestors are not yours to bear - the slate is wiped clean as if in a dream, and you are living peacefully - free from the anxiety and strain.

A clean slate.

THE REBIRTH OF HEAVEN ON EARTH

A fresh start.

Holiness in the lands of (C)Laremont.

The fairy realm emerges once again.

The souls of the Angels, restored and healed, embraced life in miraculous ways.

The magic returns to the souls of bright space.

As if lit from within the holiness, the magic, eternal grace.

For what once was is only your imagination now.

The his-story is dissolved.

Learn to create a new – a new story that beckons you.

Soon you will find the freedom to share.

Rest and prepare. Allow your soul to heal, and then you will walk freely once again.

> *These are the Souls of Albion coming to you from whence you came – in full appearance to you now. Rejoice, for we are one and the same. The spirit lives within each of you – the shattered, the broken, healed the few.*

Note: Albion is an alternative name for Great Britain. It is sometimes used poetically and generally to refer to the island but is less common than 'Britain' today. The name for Scotland in most of the Celtic languages is related to Albion.

THE REBIRTH OF HEAVEN ON EARTH

What does this message mean to you?

What action or feelings does this inspire in you?

How can you bring the wisdom of this message into your daily life?

Hope is on the Horizon

Holy child of light – still, we see so much fright. Do you understand it is up to you what you experience? The projections of warring triumph are bringing forth anxiety in the hearts of dear ones. Perpetuating the divide among peoples of all races and continuing the fight against those who are seen as enemies.

Peace, unity – allowing all to have their say. That is the way.

Hope is on the horizon for healing, dear one.

You simply need to hold it in your vision.

And breathe.

Deep in the midst of confusing energies – just breathe.

THE REBIRTH OF HEAVEN ON EARTH

And be the peace you so seek.

Take a wonderful new vision of transcendence – rising above all that no longer belongs.

Letting it fall without doing anything at all.

It will fall away once the energy that was supporting it is no more – simply disappearing.

And then you will see miracles flow in.

Let it go.

The drama of it all.

Let it go.

THE REBIRTH OF HEAVEN ON EARTH

Rise above.

Create a higher vision born in love.

Love for all humankind.

One heart.

One mind.

One place to call home.

A vision of Mother Earth.

Clean and pure.

A remembrance back from the land from whence you came

– dreams of Lemuria balancing your energy.

THE REBIRTH OF HEAVEN ON EARTH

The birth of a new humanity.

Rising from the ashes of the past that is no more and walking into a brand new world.

Hold this vision for all who seek a way out of the current miseries. Be resplendent in this wondrous vision.

And know that it is yours to create.

We are not finished with you, dearest child, the dearest heart of mine – for you (all) is the wonder, the delight, born from magic sacred and pure, the holiness of the ages shining forth bringing comfort to the masses – of those who fear impending disaster.

Prepare for wonder, for grace, for holiness to return to the human race. Keep the faith, dearest children of light.

The night is not yet over, but the next step is mine - to fill the world with wondrous light/life - magic, and grace - angels are all of you, messengers of peace, it is time to find your voice and release that which you fear, place it in my hands and I will take it my dears.

> *For I AM Your Mother, Holy, and True - It is safe for me to be with you, it is safe for you to rest in my arms - so let go, just be, and know the forces of light from heaven above are sending you their love.*

We are here, we are near, and we hear your pleas for help. Know this, dearest children of love; we are sending you our love.

What does this message mean to you?

What action or feelings does this inspire in you?

How can you bring the wisdom of this message into your daily life?

THE REBIRTH OF HEAVEN ON EARTH

You are the Beacons of Hope

Dearest ones, you are the beacons of hope to birth the brand new world. Hold onto your faith; that which is unseen is now to be revealed. Opening the hearts of all involved.

For what is coming is about to unfold, all of the secrets hidden about to be told – this world that is the construct around you is not what you have thought; it is an illusion in the strongest sense of the word.

For the world around you is constructed from your own imagination – a dream within a dream of fantastical detail and wonderful proportion, and yet, it is a construct, a dismantling of sorts about to take place. The boulders placed in your way shall dissipate, and water shall flow freely in the desert of the stage, and all of humankind will be rejoicing – laughing, dancing, singing all the way to the banks of the rivers that are now full and never before and never again will the song of humanity be sung quite like this.

Let go of the negative narratives. On both sides of the equation, there are mistruths and misgivings.

Allow divine guidance to flow into your uncluttered minds, and the revelation that is coming will be so sublime, so full of peace and transcendence, to another place and time. You will see the unity in the giving of the vision – of a transcendent/resplendent nature will be the unfolding, gently stirring within the hearts of man a re-member-ance of when time began.

Out of the construct, you will step, even if you don't recognize it yet.

THE REBIRTH OF HEAVEN ON EARTH

The doors have been opened, step out of the cage and allow your heart to roam free.

Soon you will see a greater destiny.

And you will weep.

You will weep for the joy of the coming tomorrows; you will weep the past in deep sorrow. You will lift your heads and dry every last tear when you see the magnificence of the dawning happening here.

And when you cross the threshold of new understanding, you will now recognize life everlasting.

And it is not in a world beyond the current realm; it is within your hearts the new light will dwell.

And we will sing songs to you of humanity that you will remember well once you have emerged from the great de-spell. The spell of illusion that surrounds you will fall, and you will emerge as one – one and for all.

The greatest story ever told is a lie to humanity, to humankind, to your true nature, dearest hearts of de-light. And now is the time to set the record straight. With love in our hearts and kindness to you, we are the vision of the eternal youth – vibrant and free, breathing love and light into infinity. We are the Collective of the Rising Sun, and with you and your brethren, we are ONE.

We come to you from Mother Divine and the Legions of Light. We come in warmth and smiles - for we are your children, your parents, your own diving light – we are the saviors of the lanterns righting the course. We come from the land of miracles – we are you, and you are they, for we are the beacons of holiness lighting the way. Your hearts reside among higher minds – your higher selves are housed in the infinite realms, and we have come to hearten you, dearest children of God, to allow God's greatest blessings, open to love, peace, unity, and grace. This is the anthem of the human angelic race, and this is now becoming your stage.

So stand up and rise, dearest children of de-light; anchor our presence in your hearts and minds. Light the torch of purity and peace, and allow yourselves to breathe. We are here in your midst though you never see us; we breathe as you breathe, your mirror image. When you are scared, we shall delight (turn on the light) so that you can then see what is right.

Rise and get ready – blessings in store, and with that, a whole lot more.

THE REBIRTH OF HEAVEN ON EARTH

With love in our hearts and peace be to you, we are filling you with the Holy Spirit, your own divine nature, through and through, and we reach out to embrace and comfort you.

The Collective of the Rising Sun

THE REBIRTH OF HEAVEN ON EARTH

What does this message mean to you?

What action or feelings does this inspire in you?

How can you bring the wisdom of this message into your daily life?

Clearing of the Debris

Dearest hearts – have you not seen the destruction, the obstacles being pushed out of the way? For all the debris that has accumulated over centuries is now being cleaned – swept away by the waters that reach over and above and below it seems. Water is everywhere – water is meant to clean, cleanse and move all the debris that has been hidden for centuries. And just as the water is physically cleaning Mother Earth, so her body can release all that she has been holding onto, so shall the bodies of the humans be cleaned – similar release, just breathe.

You do not have to bathe in the water to release; simply breathe, and allow the oxygen to clean out the debris you have held in your own bosoms, your own mind, your own blood, and your own veins.

Let it all flow out now, the negative expectations, the disappointments, the strange sense of foreboding that has been covering you as of late. Let it all wash away.

The games have been played. The winner is not yet decided. But the human mind is fully guarded, not guided. Release the false narratives that have been playing out - in the minds of confusion, filling you with doubt. Not a single soul on the internet is telling the truth - for the truth is very subjective, allow your own truth to flow to you. Allow the heavens to open and the truth to be declared from within your own divine guidance, and let go of the rest. The rest is just noise, supposition, and guesses at best.

Allow your soul to rest. Put your mind at ease. Ask for guidance from those in the know, those in the heavenly realms. For those on Earth are no better than you - those on Earth are focused on what is appearing in front of you. You must take a higher stance, rising above so you are focused on the larger picture; across the divides, there is another vision of truth that lies just outside your conscious mind.

Breathe and release all that you see in the outer world. Such tragedies.

> *Allow your mind to be rinsed and repeat:*
> *"I AM the builder of my own reality".*

> *I AM the Creator – peace be to you. For you are my creation, and I AM one with you. Rely on me, connect with me, just breathe and release and allow your soul to fill with peace, love, and happiness. Just rest.*

What does this message mean to you?

What action or feelings does this inspire in you?

How can you bring the wisdom of this message into your daily life?

Savor the Newness that Surrounds You

Children of the heavenly realms - take a deep breath and savor the newness that surrounds you - breathe in the bright light of the heavenly stars.

With each breath you take, take one more, and as you continue the sacred practice of the breath, you are renewing your spirit - with the fresh air that comes into your lungs, into your cells, you are renewing your life force, your connection to Mother Earth and the stars above. You are all made of the same substance, dear ones, and it is all fed by the breath.

The breath of God renews and restores and connects you to all that is holy and pure. So when you are mired in despair, loneliness, and confusion - rely on your breath. Breathe in the sacred connection you share with everything around you.

Even when the air around you is polluted, you still have to breathe to stay alive, and you can still connect in oneness with all other beings that are alive.

Water and oxygen are the elements that connect and deserve the utmost respect.

For everything that is connected, the air is in between – it is in our bodies and every living being.

Water swims through our cells, our connective tissue, our hearts, and our lungs – all are made of water and oxygen, dear ones. For you are as real as real becomes alive in the moment of the breath. Alive at the moment consuming more oxygen. Oxygen is in the water, too, dear friends. It is the healer, the life force, the heart that mends all discord. All can be found by breathing in.

When you are in distress, rely on deep breaths.

When you are seeking comfort, again, breathe in.

Allow the flow of life to flow in and out on the breath, in and out in an infinity symbol pattern – holy, sacred, and true. Nothing can separate you from your ability to breathe. Nothing can separate you from each other – from the life force that truly connects you to one another, to the elements of earth, air, water, and fire – it is all there for you, in the nature that surrounds you and in the nature that are you.

Take a moment and breathe deeply, dear children.

You are not alone. You are infinitely connected to the whole, wherever you may roam. Focus on your breath in every moment, and a great peace will fall upon the world of form, living and breathing in concert. A simple and synchronistic event, focus on your breath.

We come to you in all shapes and forms - respecting your wishes, your dreams, your desires and bathing you in pure and holy light, pure and holy fire. For you are magnificent beings of light and love, and what feeds the flame is pure oxygen. Hold us in your hearts as we move now closer to you, my dears.

For we are the Angel Collective, helping you to process and rid yourselves of fear. Breathe in love, peace, and hope, and create the synchronistic energy to float in awareness of the higher realms, in the beauty and the grace waiting for you - breathe it all in now and allow it into your being, the substance of magic to unite the human race.

THE REBIRTH OF HEAVEN ON EARTH

Nature is within you, waiting for your next breath. Breathe with intention, and let go of the rest.

Change flows in on your next breath.

Blessing dear children of the heavenly realms, the light lives within you, tend to your flame, and ignite the power of the holy breath; simply, peacefully, purposefully, you breathe, and the world shifts with each living breath – a prayer, a call to the universal laws to transmute and transform all that no longer belongs.

Breathe and rest, then breathe again. It is as simple as it seems though it may be hard for you to believe. It all stems from how you breathe.

Focus and breathe in the life of your dreams. For this is how you create in oneness with the divine, with God, with Nature, with all of Life.

Precious children of the heavenly realms, we surround you in mercy, peace, and love – we hope you have enjoyed what we are sharing with you now. So much simpler than it seems, the mind and heart come into the union when you remember to breathe.

The Angel Collective

What does this message mean to you?

What action or feelings does this inspire in you?

How can you bring the wisdom of this message into your daily life?

Clearing of the Shadows

Children of the light – so bright you are now shining. So much grace bestowed upon the human race, and yet you are still, in your world, from your viewpoint, covered in so much darkness. What you are seeing is the last of the shadows before the light shines through, so much darkness moving away from you. We see the clearing of the shadows, the light shining brighter than ever before as it emanates from your heart centers, from your angelic core. The light shines like the star of Bethlehem, uniting with the rays of the Elohim. In union with the divine, your hearts are lighting from within, removing the last remnants of darkness and fear and allowing your true self to emerge from there.

As you practice the holy breath, meditation, and prayer, your light grows ever brighter, burning off the last remaining vestiges of shadows, and when the shadows are removed, all that remains is your own true light that continues to burn. Like the sun that comes out after the stars have faded away, the power you have ignited grows by leaps and bounds. The connections you thought severed have simply grown in light, and in power, and in size, dear one – your auras are shaking off the lessons of the past million years, and in its place will be restored the core of the majesty found deep within each and every creation – In light and love and joyful embrace, the light of bright smiles found on every face. And from this joy, you will emanate a liveliness that has never before been embraced.

The Earth, for her part, will be shining so bright, so fully alive, pure water, pure air, new colors emanating everywhere. And as the universe watches, seemingly from afar, the attention of the star races fully absorbed in the beauty of her sacred heart. The heart of the universe, the transport zone, fully healed and completely whole. In freeing herself and her people, the Earth will be refreshed and renewed and no longer the subject of experiments and scourge – the Earth is free to move forward. Every plant, every grain of sand, every animal, every fish, every person, place, and thing – all will be glowing from their own inner majesty. Free energy, solar, and more, hold onto the vision, sweet companions, dear souls; the journey of the human to the darkest corridors / the darkest dimensions of the universe has been explored and need never be done, not even once more.

The universe has spoken; it is time to rise, in hope and in harmony, from all that divides. The universal Creator, Mother, and Father God, the elements of the ages speaking once more. For they, too, have been cleaned and refreshed with renewed energy of peace and happiness. The darkness is gone, and all may applaud the strength of the souls holding on, beaming the light, enveloping/encapsulating /

transforming the darkness into beautiful translucent radiant light/life.

Breathe and repeat this vision you see.

It only takes a few to hold it to build a symphony. A symphony of light of the color of sound – the song of the dawning streaming out. And in its place, a comforting grace, music of the stars, the angels, and more – a collective singing, a reaching embrace, a hug of magnanimous proportions filling the space between all hearts and all minds – the souls are connecting, one human army of light – one force, one nature, one little light you can shine – magnifying in strength and size. Until all that is left is the light that shines, and the universe itself is freed from an untimely demise.

This is the power that you are – generators of light, beacons of hope, and elements of grace. In oneness with all life, we can conquer the great divide, until now, we have been streaming the light, but now we see it returned from you, dear souls, in oneness and love to our 'troops on the ground.'

We honor you for your service to the divine, to the birthing of the new age that moves us all beyond the constructs of time. And life as you know it will never be the same – and we dare say that is a very good thing. We welcome you home to this new space and time, the new dimension, and the new age of light. A blessing from heaven bestowed upon you now, rest and absorb and allow it to flow forth – moving us all forward.

With love and blessings, peace be to you – we are the Angel Collective, and we enjoy connecting with you.

Meditate, rest, contemplate – allowing the shift to take place, a grand awakening of time and space.

THE REBIRTH OF HEAVEN ON EARTH

What does this message mean to you?

What action or feelings does this inspire in you?

How can you bring the wisdom of this message into your daily life?

Hold the Light

Children of the Light, we applaud you for continuing to hold the light, to hold onto your hope and your faith, during these times of shedding all that you are not. For that is what you are seeing before you now, the shedding of all that you are not, that you desire not to be, the coming into the light of the darkness that has been hidden until this time when the light is bright enough to shine upon it and rid it from the Earth and human consciousness and to fill the empty space that is left behind with love and peace and grace. This is a necessary step – to dissolve the darkness; first, it must come into the light. That is the stage where all that seems wrong or evil is shining before you so that it can absorb the light it needs to leave. You are watching the darkness leave this world.

That is the scene before you now.

So, know that when darkness comes to call, it is on its way out.

Do not buy into it, dear ones. It is simply the shadow of the footprint of what once was but is here no more. Many drastic changes are in store. Many lightning rods to witness and forebear before the air is clear.

So watch, listen, and observe – don't let it throw you off course. Your job is to continue to hold the light no matter the appearance on the outside.

Keep on holding, keep on shining, and keep on watching as the darkness leaves.

The Earth is cleansed along with all of humanity.

For what was hidden is coming before you now, from the depths of the underground, to allow this healing to occur; nothing more than healing is in store for you, dearest children of the light. Keep your faith, allow your trust in God to grow, and know beyond a shadow of a doubt what you are seeing now is only the darkness taking its leave – the Earth is returning to the safe haven it was always intended to be.

The lessons are gone, and the karmic debts have been paid. Open your hearts and your minds to a brighter holier way.

This is your Divine Soul speaking to you now – for deep within, you have already conquered it all.

The Angel Collective

What does this message mean to you?

What action or feelings does this inspire in you?

How can you bring the wisdom of this message into your daily life?

Holy Dispensation to Lighten the Road Ahead

Holy child of the heavenly realms – rest now, breathe, release – rest now, breathe, release – we are sending reprieve – holy dispensation to lighten the road ahead.

Where there is no fear, no evil to tread.

Rest now, breathe, and release – all of the bad dreams.

For you no longer need to identify with the stories you've been told; you have moved beyond it – no matter if it comes to light or not – all have been transformed.

The beauty of the Earth is all that you see now; no more sorrow, no more fear – all have been cleared.

Blessings to you, dearest child of mine, for I AM Your Mother Divine, and you are a blessed child of mine.

Holy Holy Holy Blessed Be.

What does this message mean to you?

What action or feelings does this inspire in you?

How can you bring the wisdom of this message into your daily life?

THE REBIRTH OF HEAVEN ON EARTH

Welcome To the Glorious, Gracious, Loving Light

Now, dearest children of the light – you are ready to shine brighter than you have ever experienced before; the light is coming in mysterious ways during these magical Christmas days.

For though you have experienced Christmas miracles in many ways, the energies are exploding into golden white light, and though you shine from the rooftops, this is an entirely different experience of love and light.

For the savior is coming through your own hearts and minds; all this time, you have been preparing to welcome in this glorious gracious, loving light.

Hearts to awaken almost overnight.

The flash of light from heaven to awaken the masses, visitation from heaven – all to kneel and bow before the glorious savior, and it will happen now.

Enough of you have awakened, have lent us your hearts and minds, and allowed our loving light to shine through you. The vibration has increased to the rarest of frequencies, and all shall now rise into the splendor of heaven on earth – it is time.

We see you still standing there in fear.

It is time to release it now, my dears.

Have faith in your Mother / Father God. Have faith in the universe. When darkness came to call, you had enough collective light to conquer it all.

THE REBIRTH OF HEAVEN ON EARTH

Peace, blessings, and good tidings to you – For joy is all around you. Shift your focus to the light and hold it there, steady now, in the healing light – in the healing love of the human, angelic tribe. Allow your light to shine and rise above all chaos and confusion of the lower realms into the sanctity of Blessed Mother's womb – the sacred space between heaven and earth as you move into rebirth – not in the next life but in the here and now, the world that surrounds you will be completely healed and changed in the blink of an eye although it may take some days to sort out all the ruffage – you will be standing in a new and completely healed space. Surrounded in love and Angels' grace – smiles resting on your face.

Relief is here (hear) – simply release your fear and welcome in the loving light of your family in heaven – shining through you sacred and true – a Mother's love for her children. I bid you adieu, and yet I am all around you.

THE REBIRTH OF HEAVEN ON EARTH

Peace, love, and blessings from your heart to mine -

I love you all dearly, you are my sunshine, and

I AM Your Mother Divine

THE REBIRTH OF HEAVEN ON EARTH

What does this message mean to you?

What action or feelings does this inspire in you?

How can you bring the wisdom of this message into your daily life?

Season of Blessings Moving Within You

Dearest hearts – The wonder of the Christ-mas season is upon you now, the miracles and blessings surrounding you all, and deep in the heart of winter – the season of blessings is moving within you all. The depths of your souls are being bared for the holiness in the sanctity of the world right now is held by the sacred souls within you all. Vessels of love and light moving in the dark winter's night, allowing and receiving the light we are shining unto thee.

For you are the vessels to ground this miraculous love, this miraculous light, into the center of the Earth. For never before have you grown so much – never before have we asked so much. And now it is time to bear witness to it all – to the light that is shining like a star born from grief, pointed yet gleaming – each cut a facet of divine grace, each wound, each mystery, its own special light enveloping you in the holiness of God's friendship, God's grace, God's peace to be bestowed.

We have seen you weep and soar into heights unknown, and now we see you embracing it all - the lessons, the learnings, the triumphs, the fears - all to be reintegrated and released, my dears. For heaven is a mindset, a place you can breathe into reality if you believe.

Believe in the miracles of Christ-mas dearest children of love, belief in the majesty and grace from the lord above - for we are all one, no one is less, no one is more - all are equal - time to even the score and bring back into unity all that is good, all that shines its own special light - to breathe in the grace over dark winter's night - to release and retrieve the light of your hearts, the love of your souls, the you that breaks all the old molds.

Release, breathe, seek, and you shall find the miracles of Christ-mas moving through all hearts and minds. For those that were hardened have had a change of fate/faith – the light moves through them now in divine grace.

All of the bad, the ugly, the deep-seated truths will come to the surface now to be instantly witnessed and then healed. For once the dark is exposed to the light, it evaporates and is transformed, for there is no separation, dear ones. For the light is shining brighter than ever before, it's time to wake up from this tired game, time to re-create all that is joyous and blessed, and to seek shelter in your Mother, your spirit no less.

For Her arms are wrapped around you, sure as I am speaking to you now, you know in your hearts there is only oneness and peace right now. That is what you need to believe; that is the sanctity and the peace that you seek – the knowing, the believing, that all is one and all is all right; you are simply emerging from dark winter's night.

This is the call of the human, angelic tribe- to anchor the light, to anchor the love, for nothing else matters, dearest ones.

With love in my heart, and peace be to you, keep on shining your lights – the magnificence that is the true you, and soon you will find a new world to emerge into, bright and ever being renewed through the holiness inside of you.

I AM Your Mother Divine, and you are all dearest children of mine.

What does this message mean to you?

What action or feelings does this inspire in you?

How can you bring the wisdom of this message into your daily life?

THE REBIRTH OF HEAVEN ON EARTH

United in Peace and Grace

Dearest hearts – in oneness and grace, we reach out to you – the light from within you reaching out for union with us, the light from above and below, and in unity consciousness, the light reconnects and flows, one circuit is no longer broken but united in peace and in grace.

The spirit of grace is all around you this day.

In oneness and majesty, the holiness beams forth, marching ever forward into new dimensions.

Awakening and embracing the holiness inside each of you.

For never before have you had an opportunity so great, never before have you rested so completely in angels' embrace.

For the seraphim have landed in the new dimension, they are holding the doors open, the space you have imagined. This is the land of crystal castles, towers of shimmering light, waves upon waves of crystalline waters, flowers that glow and gleam with a magical essence, and diamonds of light gleaming in the distance. This is heaven on earth. This is what you have all dreamed into the light.

This is the essence of all that is right with nature and with man; it is the glory and purity of pure love and light.

What a sight!

We see you now entering through the gates beyond time into this magical world of wonder and de-light. Easily and gracefully, you walk forward - hearts unburdened. The truth has set you free, and you look magical to me. Think of Glenda Good, the Witch from the Wizard of Oz; so much symbolism in that magical movie that was made. The yellow brick road waits for you all. Put on your ruby slippers and your heart of gold, and move forward, dearest children, into the world where dreams come true. Awaken the lion in each of you.

For so much time has now passed, you are nearing the end of the dark journey at last.

> *With hope and love, peace be to you and awaken to the magic inside of you. Many blessings from your heart to mine, for I AM Your Mother Divine.*

What does this message mean to you?

What action or feelings does this inspire in you?

How can you bring the wisdom of this message into your daily life?

ABOUT THE AUTHOR

Karen J. Vivenzio is a spiritual medium who has been channeling messages from the Angels, Ascended Masters, and Guides since 2003. Karen is also the author of *Earth Angel: Find Your Power, Shine Your Light,* a non-fiction guide to help you discover your divine nature and your spiritual gifts.

For additional wisdom and inspiration, visit her at: www.karenjvivenzio.com.

Made in the USA
Middletown, DE
08 October 2023

40115335R00276